A COZY
BOOK OF
HERBAL TEAS

Recipes, Remedies, and Folk Wisdom

Mindy Toomay

Prima Publishing

Design by Paula Goldstein
Composition by Archetype Book Composition
Cover design by Lindy Dunlavey, The Dunlavey Studio, Inc.
Cover illustration © Valerie Spain

Library of Congress Cataloging-in-Publication Data

Toomay, Mindy, 1951–
    A cozy book of herbal teas : recipes, remedies, and folk wisdom / Mindy Toomay.
      p. cm.
    Includes bibliographical references and index.
    ISBN 1-55958-568-4
    1. Herbal Teas.   I. Title.
TX817.T3T66   1994
641.3'57—dc20

95 96 97 RRD 10 9 8 7 6 5 4 3 2 1
Printed in the United States of America

Important Notice

The herbal teas discussed in this book are harmless when used as recommended. If you are taking prescription medications, however, check with your physician before using herbs. When you are seriously ill, or when mild symptoms persist or worsen, consult a qualified medical practitioner.

How to Order:

Single copies may be ordered from Prima Publishing, P.O. Box 1260BK, Rocklin, CA 95677; telephone (916) 632-4400. Quantity discounts are also available. On your letterhead, include information concerning the intended use of the books and the number of books you wish to purchase.

Steam rises from a cup of tea
and we are wrapped in history,
inhaling ancient times and lands,
comfort of ages in our hands.

Faith Greenbowl

To the many wise teachers, past and present,
who cultivate the qualities of wisdom,
compassion, and joy.
And to organic gardeners everywhere,
who nurture healthy life.

Contents

Acknowledgments

I feel deep appreciation for my husband, Tad, who eagerly helped with the research for this book and reviewed the manuscript with a careful and caring eye. He has loved me and supported this project steadfastly—such a gift. Miriam Davis also read the manuscript and offered important feedback. Thank you, friend.

Tremendous thanks to Anna Moore, who made her home, computer, and herbal library available to me for the duration of this project. Largely due to her generosity, these last months have been focused and cozy.

My heartfelt thanks go also to Candis Cantin Packard, herbalist extraordinaire, who reviewed the medicinal tea section and helped refine the remedies.

Thanks to Andi Reese-Brady, able project editor, for her enthusiasm and flexibility. She and page designer Paula Goldstein listened to my sometimes vague ideas and incorporated them into the finished book, for which I am grateful. Lindy Dunlavey of Dunlavey Studios performed her magic once again and designed a cover that conveys great fun and vitality—I salute you, Lindy.

Finally, a thousand thanks to Jennifer Basye Sander, my editor at Prima Publishing, whose instincts told her I should write a book about herbal teas. She planted the seed that sank roots, flourished, and blossomed as this book.

INTRODUCTION

There is something about the very act of making herbal tea that is restful, even healing. We slow down to measure out herbs. We notice the cool smoothness of the pottery as we take it from its shelf. We pause and reflect for a peaceful moment while waiting for the kettle to boil and the herbs to steep. And then we sit, already soothed by the simple ritual, and sip the brew—inhaling its aroma, relishing the warmth cradled in our hands. The entire process is a blessed respite from hurry and strife, and a refreshing celebration of the senses.

I encountered the notion that herbs are suitable for making tea during my early study of health and nutrition. Chamomile was my first experiment in this vein, and the tea made from these sunny flowers is still a personal favorite. I happily moved on through the mints, added ginger and cinnamon, then discovered the citrus-flavored herbs: lemongrass, verbena, and balm. I began experimenting with blends and filled dozens of canning jars with various concoctions to share with friends.

Herbal teas became a fun and inexpensive hobby that brought a great deal of cozy companionship to those years. And the herbs brought healing, as well. My explorations included tea therapy when minor ailments cropped up—peppermint for indigestion, hops for insomnia, yellow dock for a skin rash. As a simple refreshment or a mild medicine, herbal teas eventually became a part of my daily life.

I took up drinking coffee in my twenties, and I enjoy a strong cup of it, black and bracing, when my sleepy brain wants a jolt. But my passion for herbal teas has endured. I rejoice in the precious times—alone or with friends—when there is no rush, nothing pressing to do. Then I brew and sip a cup of herbal tea, and retreat from the world for awhile. Resting in the quiet of these moments, I am renewed.

This book is for everyone who is thirsting for quiet times to ease the stress; for a rare, tranquil kind of aliveness. I invite you to pause and enjoy a cozy cup of calm.

One sip of this will bathe the drooping spirits in delight, beyond the bliss of dreams.

—Milton

I invite you magnanimously
to please be my guest for tea
at a room with high standards of taste
where the hostess remembers my face
and greets me by name at the door
and recalls what I've ordered before
and inquires kindly after my day,
and appreciates all that I say.

She'll have orange pekoe for the pot
and darjeeling, as likely as not,
or if you are not in the pink
our hostess knows which herbs to drink,
like ginger to help with the grippe
mixed with cinnamon and the rose hip;
or fresh lemon balm if you wish,
perhaps blended with sweet licorice.

So whether you feel well or ill
this refreshment will quite fit the bill
and, of course, you will quite enjoy me.
Yours truly. RSVP.

—Aubrey Henslowe

A SIMPLE GUIDE TO BREWING HERBAL TEAS

Basic Principle of Herbal Tea

When the leaves, seeds, roots, and fruits of herbs meet very hot water, their volatile oils—which contain the aroma, taste, and medicinal value of the plant—are released. The essence of the herb is transferred to the water, to be sipped by us and incorporated into our bodies, for sheer enjoyment or for healing.

Basic Terms and Techniques

Herb

Technically, an herb is a nonwoody plant that dies down to the ground after it has flowered. In general usage, however, any plant used for medicine, seasoning, dye, or cosmetic purposes is called an herb.

Decoction

Roots, seeds, barks, and extremely coarse leaves must be boiled for a time to release their active ingredients. Generally, herbalists recommend adding the herb to the water after it has reached the boiling point. Then the heat is reduced, and the herb is simmered in the pan—uncovered—for about 10–20 minutes. The water in the pan will be reduced by about half, which concentrates the herb's flavor and potency.

Polly put the kettle on, we'll all have tea.

—Charles Dickens

6

Infusion

Delicate leaves and blossoms should not be boiled, as their aromatic oils are quickly released and easily evaporated. For infusions, the just-boiled water is poured over the herbs in a warmed teapot, the lid is put in place, and the herbs are allowed to steep for 3–10 minutes, depending on the herb and your personal taste.

The words *infusion* and *tisane* are sometimes used interchangeably in herbals. *Tisane* is simply the French term for the same preparation.

Combining Decoction and Infusion

Some recipes combine coarse plant parts, which are usually decocted, with finer parts, which are usually infused. In such cases, make the decoction first. After the designated simmering time has elapsed, strain the decoction and pour the liquid over the remaining herbs in a teapot. Infuse for the designated time, strain, and serve.

Essential Tools

✧ You will want to acquire *glass or ceramic jars* with tight-fitting lids to store dried herbs and spices. Used jars are fine, as long as they are thoroughly washed and dried before packing with herbs. Labeling the jars is very helpful, as the dried leaves of many herbs look practically identical.

✧ Many people use a perforated metal ball, called an infuser, to brew herbal teas. The herbs are placed in the infuser, the ball is latched and inserted in the teapot, and the hot water is poured in. Herbs release their flavors more readily, however, when they are allowed plenty of room to move about in the water, so I prefer not to stuff them into an infuser. I usually put the loose herbs directly in the teapot, pour in the boiling water, cover the pot, and steep. I then strain the tea through a *bamboo or wire mesh strainer* into warmed cups or into a separate teapot for serving. An infuser can be useful for brewing a single cup of tea for which you are using only a teaspoon or so of herbs. Place a plate over the cup while the tea is steeping to prevent evaporation of the herb's aromatic oils. Use an *infuser made of bamboo or stainless steel,* not aluminum. Some teapots come with a built-in, removable infuser, which is a very handy feature.

✧ Dried roots, seeds, and barks are sometimes crushed or ground before brewing. A *mortar and pestle* are the best tools for these jobs.

✧ A *glass or enameled pan* should be used for boiling the water, to avoid a metallic taste in the tea. Stainless steel is acceptable for making herbal teas; aluminum and cast iron are not. The active ingredients of the herbs can react with the metal in the pan, potentially altering flavor in the case of beverage herbs or effectiveness in the case of medicinal ones.

✧ Likewise, a *ceramic or enameled teapot* is preferable to metal ones. The teapot must have a lid, which is kept in place throughout the steeping time. This way, the herb's aromatic oils will condense inside the pot and be recaptured by the tea rather than evaporating into the air.

✧ Herbal teas may be served in any *glass or ceramic cup* of your choosing.

Helpful Tips

✧ Use spring water or distilled water for best results, heated to the boiling point, but not overboiled. Too much boiling concentrates the minerals in the water, which can affect the taste.

✧ To take the chill off the teapot, swirl some hot water in it before adding the herbs. A tea cozy placed over the pot will keep the contents warm for long periods if the tea is not finished immediately.

The cozy fire is bright and gay, the merry kettle boils away and hums a cheerful song. I sing the saucer and the cup; pray, Mary, fill the teapot up, and do not make it strong.
—Barry Pain

- Generally, the herbs should be strained out immediately after decocting or infusing. Oversteeping can bring out the bitterness of some herbs. The strained tea can be refrigerated in a closed glass container for up to 3 days. Reheat herb teas very gently on the stovetop in a covered glass or enameled pan.

- After making tea for the first time with a particular herb, you may decide you want its flavor to be stronger. It is preferable to intensify the tea's flavor by using more of the herb rather than by steeping for a longer period of time. Again, oversteeping may bring out the herb's bitter quality.

- Fresh herbs may be wrapped in a clean tea towel and gently pounded with a wooden spoon to release their aromatic oils before adding to the pot.

- Increase the proportion of herb to water if a tea is to be served iced, since the melting ice will dilute the beverage tea. Strain the tea after brewing and cool in the refrigerator before pouring over ice.

- Teas may be sweetened with honey, if desired, to achieve a pleasant taste. Add the honey while the tea is hot so it will dissolve easily. Milk is not added to herbal teas, as it can mask more delicate flavors.

chapter TWO

HERBAL TEAS AS PLEASING BEVERAGES

Since our distant beginnings, still shrouded in mystery, humans have depended on plants. Certain plants were so fundamental to the well-being of ancient civilizations that they were revered as sacred gifts from the gods.

Many things have changed in the last few million years, but a few simple facts have not. We still rely on plants, and they continue to provide abundantly for our nourishment, enjoyment, and healing.

In chapter five (page 63) I will discuss the healing properties of herbs. But in this chapter, we are concerned only with pleasure, and herbs do not disappoint.

A Beverage Primer

All beverages—except plain water and the milk of various animals—are derived from plants. This is a testament to the diversity of aromas and flavors offered by the plant species and to the creative imaginations of human beings, who continue to explore the nearly infinite possibilities of tea.

The simplest—and perhaps, therefore, most wonderful—plant beverages are herbal teas. No complicated procedure is required to make them, and the herbs themselves are inexpensive and often delicious. Herbal tea is an economical, cozy, homespun delight.

Occasionally, I serve black Russian tea, but mostly China greens, with beautiful names. I also serve herbal teas made of many leaves and blossoms.

—M.F.K. Fisher

The aromas and tastes of herbs range from sweet to spicy, mellow to intense, earthy to ethereal. Some herbs make deliciously satisfying teas or effective medicines when put all alone into the pot: chamomile, peppermint, and linden are three such classics. The real fun of beverage teas, though, is in mingling two or more herbs in the pot—balancing their flavors, aromas, and colors just to your liking.

The Art of Herbal Tea Design

It is great fun to brew small cups of a dozen or so herbs and concoct your own blends, combining small amounts of this and that to find out what you like. Be sure to label the cups and take good notes. Life in the laboratory can be confusing, and you don't want to forget how you arrived at the very best tea you've ever tasted.

The art of designing herbal teas involves our senses of sight and smell, as well as taste. The best teas are appetizing in color and emit tantalizing fragrances that greatly enhance the sipping experience. Your most important tea-design considerations are, therefore, the following:

✧ FLAVOR. Your primary concerns in the flavor realm are *body* and *balance*. A good tea must have good body, meaning its taste must be distinctly herbaceous and mouth-filling.

Balance is equally important. When herbs are blended expertly, no single flavor dominates. Each of the herbs provides a flavor note, and the result is a satisfying harmony. A tea that comes across as predominantly sweet or bitter, without any distinguishing complexity, is destined for the drain.

⬦ AROMA. The fragrance of an herbal tea is at least half of our enjoyment. Its aroma should be rich and pleasant, not musty or bland. If a tea doesn't smell inviting, it's unlikely to taste good. Let your nose be your guide in the blending process.

⬦ COLOR. Most herbal teas range from sunny yellow to greenish or reddish brown in color. One or another of these colors can be emphasized, as you wish. Most important, the appearance of the tea should be clear, not cloudy, and its color vivid. Color density is closely related to the strength of the brew—too pale and the tea is likely to taste bland and watery; too dark or cloudy and you may have a palate-numbing sludge in the cup.

There are no hard and fast rules about how much of an herb to use. Let taste be your guide. I find that 2–3 teaspoons of dried leaves or flowers to a cup of water is about

Smell is a potent wizard that transports us across thousands of miles and all the years we have lived.

—Helen Keller

14

right for my tastes (leaves and flowers are termed aerial parts in the herbal lexicon). With barks, seeds, and roots, I usually use a little less.

Brewing time will also vary, depending on the depth of flavor you prefer. Five minutes is usually long enough to get the best flavors from an herb's delicate aerial parts; roots, seeds, and barks are coarser and will require more time in the water, usually 10–15 minutes. If you want to intensify the flavor of the tea, it is better to begin with more herbs in the pot than to increase the steeping time. Remember that oversteeping can leach an unpleasant bitterness from many herbs. (For more tips on the brewing process, see chapter one, A Simple Guide to Brewing Herbal Teas.)

When you have discovered a blend you particularly enjoy, you may wish to mix up a big batch of the component herbs in exact proportions and place them in an airtight jar for storage. Make up a name for the tea, if you wish, and label the jar accordingly. Store the blend in a cool, dark place. For future reference, keep a notebook specifying the herbs that make up the blend and their proportions. Each time you make the tea, shake the jar and turn it upside down a few times to properly combine the herbs before measuring them out.

Sun Tea

The sun provides sufficient heat to brew a tasty tea. Place the herbs in a large glass jar, add an appropriate amount of cool spring water, cover tightly, and place the jar in a spot outdoors where it will receive 3 to 6 hours of direct sunlight. Test the tea after 3 hours and allow it to steep longer if you desire a stronger flavor. When the tea is brewed to your liking, strain off the herbs and refrigerate the tea in a closed glass container. Serve cold, with or without ice.

If you intend to serve a tea iced, remember that it should be brewed slightly stronger than if you were serving it hot, since melting ice will dilute its flavor in the glass.

Tea Sweeteners

Honey is the hands-down winner in any taste test of herbal tea sweeteners. Any sweetener can mask rather than enhance herbal flavors, so start with just a thin film of honey on the spoon, stir it into the tea, and taste. Honey becomes another flavor element that will change the taste of the tea—remember, flavor balance is the goal. The more you come to appreciate the subtle flavors of the herbs themselves, the less inclined you will be to sweeten the tea, unless you are deliberately looking for a balancing flavor for the bitter or sour herbs.

Love and scandal are the best sweeteners of tea.
—Henry Fielding

Many herbs come across as faintly sweet in the cup, but two particular herbs deserve special mention for their sweetening abilities. Licorice contains a substance said to be 50 times sweeter than table sugar, and a humble little herb called stevia is much sweeter even than that. These herbs can be used in blends to provide a sweet note, but use a light hand. The flavor of stevia, in particular, can be cloying if too much is added.

An Introduction to the Blends

In the pages that follow, I offer ten of my personal favorite herb tea blends. In the case of beverage teas, providing precise recipes is a bit silly because herbs can taste slightly different from region to region or season to season and because personal preference is the only true guide to preparing a great herb blend. My hope is that these favorites of mine will excite you about the vast possibilities and that you will begin to design herbal teas that perfectly satisfy your own tastes.

In my recipes, leaves, flowers, and chopped roots are measured by the *rounded* teaspoon, seeds and powders by the *level* teaspoon. About 3 times the volume of fresh herb may be substituted for dried herb amounts. Fresh herbs should be loosely mounded in the measuring spoon, not packed.

After the Boston Tea Party made the drinking of imported teas politically incorrect, colonists began to brew beverages from indigenous plants. The tradition of "liberty teas" was born.

Each of the following recipes yields enough tea for 2 cozy cups. If you are preparing tea for several people, multiply the herb and water amounts accordingly.

A selection of teatime treats is presented in chapter four, for inspiration when you are planning a tea social. Any of your favorite cakes and cookies will probably taste delicious with herbal teas, though I have found that strong flavors such as chocolate can overpower the more delicate herb teas.

Notes on ten of my favorite tasty tea herbs are presented in chapter three. Their names appear in capital letters in the recipes below. I hope that knowing a little about these herbs will add to your enjoyment of the teas made from them.

Flower Power

Some of my favorite tea blossoms combine to create this fragrant, delicate sipping tea. A touch of spicy cloves anchors the ethereal floral flavors. Flowers being what they are, this is a wonderful tea for easing the mind and lifting the spirits.

SERVES 2

2 teaspoons dried CHAMOMILE flowers
1 1/2 teaspoons dried LAVENDER flowers
1 teaspoon dried elder flowers
1/8 teaspoon powdered cloves
2 cups water, barely boiled

Place all the herbs directly into the teapot. Pour the boiling water over them, cover the pot, and steep 5 minutes. Strain and sweeten with honey, if desired. Serve hot.

Sweet Stability

In this warming tea blend, the almost heavy sweetness of licorice is balanced by the uplifting flavors of orange peel and catnip. Caraway fills out the tea's body. This tea helps bring me back to earth when I'm feeling a bit ungrounded. (Licorice root tea is not recommended for people prone to high blood pressure, pregnant women, or women with fibroids.)

SERVES 2

2 1/2 cups water
1/4 teaspoon dried LICORICE root
1 teaspoon dried caraway seeds, crushed
2 teaspoons dried orange peel, crushed
2 teaspoons dried catnip leaves

Bring the water to a boil in a glass or stainless steel pan over high heat. Add the licorice root, caraway seeds, and orange peel, reduce heat to medium, and simmer, uncovered, 5 minutes. Meanwhile, place the catnip in the teapot. When simmering time is up, pour the unstrained decoction into the teapot, cover, and steep about 5 minutes. Strain and serve hot, or chill and serve over ice.

Rose Blush

This lively tea has a wonderful fragrance, flavor, and color. Hot or iced, it refreshes the senses and soothes the spirit.

SERVES 2

2 teaspoons dried rose petals
1 teaspoon crushed dried rose hips
1 teaspoon dried sage
1 small dried hibiscus flower
2 cups water, barely boiled

Combine the herbs in a teapot. Add the boiling water, cover, and steep 7–10 minutes. Strain and sweeten with honey to taste. Serve hot, or chill and serve over ice with a fresh mint sprig garnishing the glass.

Journey to Antiquity

Of all the herbs I use for tea, ginger most clearly evokes faraway times and places. Rose hips and aniseed, too, have long and colorful histories. This is the tea I drink to steep myself in the mysteries of the past. It is my husband's all-time favorite herbal tea.

SERVES 2

3 cups water
2 1/4-inch slices fresh GINGER root
2 teaspoons crushed dried rose hips
1 teaspoon dried aniseed, crushed

Bring the water to a boil in a glass or stainless steel pan over high heat. Meanwhile, cut the ginger into 1/4-inch slices and hit each slice gently with the broad side of a knife to break up the pulp a bit. Add the herbs to the boiling water, reduce heat to medium, and simmer, uncovered, 5 minutes. Strain and sweeten to taste with honey. Serve hot or chill and serve over ice.

Taste of the Forest

The delicious, pine-like flavor of rosemary inspired this blend. I find it quite delicious unsweetened, though honey can be added if desired. This tea pairs perfectly with rose-petal jam on toast. I recommend using fresh rosemary and bay, since their flavors are less satisfying when dried and the fresh herbs are widely available.

SERVES 2

2 teaspoons fresh ROSEMARY leaves, bruised
1 teaspoon dried juniper berries, crushed
1 teaspoon dried PEPPERMINT leaves
1 small fresh bay leaf (Laurus nobilis), bruised
2 cups water, barely boiled

Place all the herbs directly into the teapot. Pour the boiling water over them, cover the pot, and steep 5 minutes. Strain and sweeten with honey to taste, if desired. Serve hot or chill and serve over ice.

There's rosemary, that's for remembrance; pray you love, remember.

—William Shakespeare

Sail Away

To me, this tea tastes deliciously exotic. I crave it when I want to momentarily escape the mundane. Hibiscus flowers have a pleasant but sour taste that combines well with the sweet spices.

SERVES 2

2 1/2 cups water
1 teaspoon dried fenugreek seeds
1 small dried hibiscus flower
1/4 teaspoon powdered cardamom
1/4 teaspoon powdered CINNAMON

Bring the water to a boil in a glass or stainless steel pan over hight heat. Add the fenugreek, reduce heat to medium, and simmer uncovered for 5 minutes. Place the cardamom, cinnamon, and hibiscus into the teapot. Pour the fenugreek decoction over the herbs, cover the pot, and steep 5 minutes. Strain and sweeten with honey to taste. Serve hot, or chill and serve over ice.

A Continental Cup

Linden is a favored tea herb in Europe, where harvesters are said to stand on very tall ladders to reach the best-tasting blossoms at the very tops of the trees. All by itself, linden makes a wonderful tea, but I also enjoy it combined with the peppery taste of hyssop and the mellow tang of lemon balm.

1 tablespoon dried linden flowers
2 teaspoons dried HYSSOP leaves
1 tablespoon fresh LEMON BALM leaves
2 cups water, barely boiled

Place all the herbs directly into the teapot. Pour the boiling water over them, cover the pot, and steep 5 minutes. Strain and sweeten with honey to taste, if desired. Serve hot.

Sonoma Meadow

This tea calls to mind the beauty of the coastal meadows near my home in northern California. Sit back with your feet up, close your eyes, and be transported to the countryside by the fragrance and flavor of this soothing brew.

Serves 2

1 teaspoon dried red clover
1 teaspoon dried CHAMOMILE flowers
1 teaspoon dried marshmallow root
1 1/2 teaspoons dried FENNEL seed, crushed
2 cups water, barely boiled

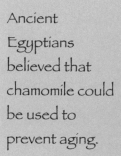

Ancient Egyptians believed that chamomile could be used to prevent aging.

Place all the herbs directly into the teapot. Pour the boiling water over the herbs, cover the pot, and steep 10 minutes. Strain and sweeten with honey to taste. Serve hot, or chill and serve over ice.

Sarsaparilla Samba

Root beer tea, anyone? Sarsaparilla gives this tea its characteristic root beer flavor, with spearmint and pepper livening things up.

SERVES 2

1 tablespoon plus 1 teaspoon dried sarsaparilla root
2 teaspoons dried spearmint leaves
8 black peppercorns, crushed
2 cups water, barely boiled

Place all the herbs directly into the teapot. Pour the water over them, cover the pot, and steep 15 minutes. Strain and serve hot or chill and serve over ice.

Very Berry Blend

This tea is a lovely pale pink and wonderfully aromatic. The honey is essential, since it balances the tartness of the berries and lemon. Buy a basket of raspberries, use several to make the tea, and mash the remainder to spread on warm cinnamon toast. Serve the toast alongside the tea for a wonderful breakfast or late afternoon snack.

SERVES 2

2 ounces fresh raspberries (about 1/2 cup)
2 teaspoons dried LEMONGRASS
2 teaspoons dried strawberry leaves
1 teaspoon dried HYSSOP leaves
1 teaspoon honey, or to taste
2 cups water, barely boiled

Place the fresh berries directly into the teapot and mash lightly with a fork. Add the lemongrass, strawberry leaves, and hyssop. Pour the boiling water over the herbs, cover the pot, and steep 10 minutes. Strain, stir in the honey until dissolved, and serve hot.

"Have some wine," the March Hare said in an encouraging tone. Alice looked all round the table, but there was nothing on it but tea. "I don't see any wine," she remarked. "There isn't any," said the March Hare.

—Lewis Carroll

chapter
THREE

TASTY HERBS FOR TEAS

Hundreds of herbs have been used to brew beverages and medicinal teas throughout recorded history. A few herbs have been particularly favored since antiquity and are essentials in every herbal tea pantry. Chamomile, licorice, and peppermint, for instance, were lavishly praised in the herbals of old and are prominent in modern herbals, as well. These classic herbs are included in this chapter, but not out of any sense of duty to tradition. They are, quite simply, among the most delicious of herbs. That they also offer time-tested medicinal benefits is a generous bonus.

To develop a full appreciation of the art and science of herbology, explore the world of herbs in books. A browse through the antiquated herbals at reference libraries can provide a fascinating glimpse at the social and medical practices of ages past. For practical guidance, look to the more modern herbals. A brief reading list for further study appears on page 117. Any herb shop or library can make many additional recommendations.

This selection of Tasty Herbs for Teas is admittedly subjective. These are the herbs I like best and use most frequently. The herbal tea experiments that happen in *your* kitchen will reveal your own personal favorites.

Chamomile

ROMAN VARIETY: ANTHEMIS NOBILIS, *also known as*
    CHAMAEMELUM NOBILE

GERMAN OR WILD VARIETY: MATRICARIA CHAMOMILLA

Flavor

The fragrance and flavor of chamomile are often described as faintly applelike. These qualities are reflected in its botanical name, derived from the Greek *kamai,* "on the ground," and *melon,* "apple." Groundapple has long been one of its colloquial names. Chamomile tea is wonderful hot and lends a cooling quality to summer iced teas.

History and Folklore

✦ The sweet fragrance of this golden flower symbolized humility to the ancient Greeks and made chamomile a popular herb in medieval times for "strewing"—scattering about the place to mask unpleasant odors.

✦ So highly prized was chamomile by the early Anglo-Saxons that they considered it one of nine sacred herbs given to the world by the god Woden.

✦ In Beatrix Potter's wonderful *Tales of Peter Rabbit,* Peter's mother lovingly ministers to his aching head with a cup of

> Like a chamomile bed, the more it is trodden the more it will spread.
> —Old English proverb

hot chamomile tea. Quite soon, he is fit once again for garden-raiding.

Modern Uses
Chamomile's medicinal benefits have been chronicled for centuries. To this day it is widely prescribed by herbalists as a gentle sedative and is commonly used to help relieve poor digestion, headaches, fevers, colds and flu, menstrual pain, urinary tract problems, morning sickness, and colitis.

Cautions
A member of the daisy family, chamomile is related to ragweed. It has no known toxicity but should be avoided by people with sensitivities to ragweed.

Botanical Notes
Chamomile is an evergreen perennial, suitable for sunny spots or partial shade. It may be propagated by seed or by root division. Sow seeds in the spring after the last frost. *Anthemis nobilis* is the species prized for tea. Flower buds are the flavorful plant parts harvested for beverage and medicinal teas.

Known as "the plant's physician," chamomile has a reputation for reviving and strengthening neighboring plants. It is also widely believed that chamomile and its daisy cousins attract beneficial predatory insects to the garden.

Cinnamon

CINNAMOM ZEYLANICUM

Flavor

Cinnamon delivers a wonderful balance of sweet and hot flavors. Its spiciness is stimulating, though not overly warming. I often find that a pinch of cinnamon rounds out a tea blend perfectly. It is a powerful spice, however, so use very small amounts unless you want its taste to dominate.

History and Folklore

✧ Drawing an analogy between the human body and a tree, ancient herbalists believed cinnamon bark from the trunk of the tree effective in treating ailments of the torso, while twigs were preferred for treating the extremities.

✧ In Chinese medicine, the twigs and bark of a very closely related tree, *Cinnamon cassia*, are highly regarded as healing aids. *C. cassia* is very similar in taste and appearance to *C. zeylanicum*.

Modern Uses

Cinnamon is a wonderful culinary spice. Its sweet/spicy punch is particularly useful in desserts. It is most commonly prescribed

There is a tale of cinnamon growing around marshes under the protection of a terrible kind of bat . . . invented by the natives to raise the price.
—Pliny the Elder,
A.D. 77

31

by herbalists as a remedy for nausea, indigestion, diarrhea, and circulation problems.

Cautions
Cinnamon should be used very sparingly by pregnant women, as it is believed to be a uterine stimulant.

Botanical Notes
The spice is the dried inner bark of this evergreen tropical tree. Pieces of bark curl as they dry, forming the familiar cinnamon sticks, sometimes called "quills."

Fennel
FOENICULUM VULGARE

Flavor
Fennel has a mild licoricelike flavor that lends a warming, slightly sweet note to teas.

History and Folklore
✧ In medieval times, people chewed on fennel seeds on fast days to appease their appetites.
✧ To the ancient Greeks, fennel symbolized success.

Modern Uses

Fennel is a culinary herb in good standing. The leaves, picked before the plant flowers, make a tasty addition to salads or stir-fries. The seeds add a distinctive note to simmered soups and sauces. The bulbous stem of a particular fennel variety is a vegetable favored in Italian cooking. In the medicinal realm, modern herbalists prescribe fennel tea as a stomach soother and occasionally as an herb that increases the flow of milk in nursing mothers.

Cautions

Some people are allergic to fennel oil in its concentrated form, but using the whole seed in teas rarely poses a problem.

Botanical Notes

Fennel is a member of the *Umbelliferae* genus, along with dill, anise, caraway, and several other common herbs. It is a perennial plant that grows wild in Asia minor and in some parts of the United States and Europe. Home gardeners usually cultivate it as an annual. The feathery leaves should be harvested before the plant flowers and are best used fresh. Harvest seeds in late summer.

> Above the lowly plant it towers, the fennel with its yellow flowers, and in an earlier age than ours was gifted with the wondrous powers lost vision to restore.
>
> —Henry Wadsworth Longfellow

33

Ginger
ZINGEBER OFFICINALE

Flavor

Ginger delivers a spicy tang with a hint of sweetness. It is a complex and delicious seasoning that can taste quite hot when used liberally in cooking, as it is in the cuisine of Thailand.

History and Folklore

✦ By 1884, ginger was so popular in Great Britain that over five million pounds were imported that year alone.

✦ Gingerbread is commonly believed to be an invention of the American South. Not so! The ancient Greeks were enjoying gingerbread 4,000 years ago.

Modern Uses

Ginger is an important seasoning in the cuisines of the Far East. In the United States, dried and powdered ginger is a popular spice used in baked desserts. Candied, or crystallized, ginger is enjoyed in many parts of the world as a component in desserts.

Medicinally, ginger is used to good effect to combat colds, to soothe the stomach, and to promote circulation.

Nose, nose, jolly red nose, who gave thee this jolly red nose? . . . Nutmegs and ginger, cinnamon and cloves, and they gave me this jolly red nose.

—Francis Beaumont

34

Cautions

Ginger should be used judiciously by women in the early months of pregnancy.

Botanical Notes

Ginger is a perennial plant indigenous to Asia and cultivated throughout the tropics. The knobby and branched root is the useful part of the plant. Ginger can be grown successfully by home gardeners in Florida, where tropical conditions can be duplicated. The rest of us can buy plump, juicy-looking roots from the grocer and store them in an airtight container in the refrigerator. The root will stay fresh for weeks under these conditions. However, I buy it in small quantities and replenish my supply regularly at the produce market.

Hyssop
HYSSOPUS OFFICINALIS

Flavor

Hyssop has a mildly peppery, somewhat camphorous taste. Its flavor is not particularly satisfying when brewed alone, but I consider it a wonderful blending herb.

History and Folklore

- ✧ Hyssop baths are an old English remedy for rheumatism.
- ✧ Hyssop was a holy herb to the Hebrews, used to cleanse and freshen sacred places. It was also favored in medieval times as a strewing herb, along with the mints, lavender, and chamomile.

Modern Uses

Oil of hyssop is a constituent in the popular liqueur known as Chartreuse and is used in perfume-making. In Europe, hyssop is valued as a culinary, as well as medicinal, herb. Medicinally, hyssop tea is most frequently prescribed for indigestion and ailments of the lungs, such as asthma.

Cautions

Hyssop has no known contraindications.

Botanical Notes

Hyssop is a semievergreen perennial shrub, beautiful in form and fragrant of leaf and flower. It is of the Labiatae family, and therefore related to rosemary, thyme, and lavender. It makes a fine clipped hedge when shaped in the early spring; unclipped, it develops an attractive spreading habit but should be cut back occasionally to restore its shape. The pretty flowers are most often deep blue in color and are highly attractive to bees.

Lavender

LAVENDULA VERA *or* L. OFFICINALIS

Flavor

The aroma and flavor of lavender are cooling, slightly resinous, and intensely floral.

History and Folklore

- In the Middle Ages—an exceedingly romantic time—lavender was considered an herb of love. Its aphrodisiacal powers were legendary.
- Lavender was another medieval strewing herb, used particularly to freshen the air in sickrooms.
- Seventeenth-century herbalist John Parkinson considered lavender to be "especially good use for all griefes and paines of the head and brain."

Modern Uses

Lavender is a popular scent for soaps, cosmetics, and potpourris, as it has been since the days of the ancient Greeks and Romans.

Medicinally, lavender tea is most often used for its calmative effects in sleep aids and digestive remedies. The heady, camphorous perfume of lavender is considered beneficial to alleviate headaches and allay lightheadedness.

Lavender, in its blue dress, is the wonder and joy of the south, and its scent is God's gift to earth.

—Maurice Mességué

Lavender flowers are considered safe for internal use, though highly sensitive people may experience allergic reactions.

Botanical Notes
There are a great many varieties of the genus *Lavendula,* cultivated primarily in Europe and the United States. The useful part of the plant is the pale purple flowers that bloom in the summer. The foliage is a dusty silver-green. Lavender is a very popular herb among home gardeners.

Lemon Balm
MELISSA OFFICINALIS

Flavor
Lemon balm, as its common name implies, tastes mildly tart and lemony. It lends a refreshing, slightly minty quality to tea blends and is also enjoyable steeped as a "simple"—a tea made from a single herb.

History and Folklore
- Lemon balm was one of the prized plants in Thomas Jefferson's garden at Montecello.
- Bee keepers of old would rub lemon balm leaves inside a hive to preserve the colony. Pliny observed this attribute of

the herb some 2,000 years ago. The Latin name *Melissa* is derived from the Greek word for the honey bee.

✧ Though lemon balm's fragrance is pleasant to bees, other insects are thought to dislike it, hence its historical use as an insect repellent.

✧ To the ancient Greeks, lemon balm signified sympathy.

✧ Lemon balm is considered a cheering herb, and it has been included in "elixirs of youth" throughout the ages.

Modern Uses

Fresh lemon balm leaves will add a pleasant zip to fresh salads. Medicinally, it is prescribed for the treatment of depression, nervous conditions, and indigestion. Some natural healers believe it has the same tonic properties as honey or royal jelly. The aromatic oils of lemon balm are easily lost, so fresh leaves are considered far superior to dried.

Cautions

Lemon balm is mild in effect and considered quite safe.

Botanical Notes

Melissa is a highly fragrant perennial plant, a member of the mint family. It is considered homely by many gardeners but is still cultivated for its pleasing perfume. The light-green leaves

> Balm is sovereign for the brain, strengthening the memory and powerfully chasing away melancholy.
> —John Evelyn, 1679

are the useful and fragrant part of the plant; its white flowers are insignificant. The plant is highly attractive to bees.

Licorice
GLYCYRRHIZA

Flavor

Licorice contains a substance that is 50 times as sweet as table sugar. Licorice provides a full, almost heavy sweetness to teas. Some people enjoy it alone, though it combines well with many other herbs.

History and Folklore

⬧ Licorice has been used medicinally for at least 2,500 years and is still included in the official U.S. Pharmacopoeia as an effective treatment for stomach ulcers.

⬧ In China, *G. uralenis*—"gan cao"—is called "the great detoxifier" and is used to drive poisons from the system. In the Chinese system of medicine, licorice is considered "the grandfather of herbs."

Modern Uses

Licorice is occasionally used in cooking to lend an exotic sweet flavor to desserts. In gel form, licorice has long been a favorite candy treat.

Medicinally, licorice is known to neutralize stomach acidity, making it an effective treatment for stomach ulcers. Chewing on dried licorice root can help to appease the appetite when a weight-loss diet is undertaken. It tastes satisfyingly sweet but contains almost no calories. Licorice tea is sometimes recommended for bronchial and urinary tract problems.

Cautions

Some herbalists feel that licorice in therapeutic doses is best avoided by people prone to high blood pressure because it may cause fluid retention. It is also best avoided by those with a rapid heartbeat and those taking digoxin-based drugs. It is not recommended for pregnant women or women with fibroids.

Botanical Notes

Licorice is a perennial plant that grows wild in parts of Europe and Asia. Spain is the principal exporter of stick licorice. The woody root is wrinkled and brown on the outside and yellow on the inside.

Peppermint
MENTHA PIPERITA

Flavor

Peppermint has a cool, clean, refreshing flavor that is slightly spicy and faintly fruity.

History and Folklore

✧ Myth has it that Persephone, jealous wife of Pluto, discovered her husband in the arms of a beautiful nymph named Minthe. In a rage, she changed Minthe into a lowly shrub. Not even Pluto could undo the spell, but he made the plant highly aromatic so that Minthe's sweetness would be preserved.

✧ Peppermint was another important strewing herb in medieval times, used to freshen the air in kitchens and sickrooms.

✧ To the ancient Greeks, mint symbolized hospitality.

✧ Japanese mint and peppermint are the sources of menthol, the important ingredient in so many soothing balms.

✧ Athletes in ancient Rome perfumed their bodies with mint leaves, believing that this increased their strength.

Modern Uses

Peppermint is a popular flavoring for candy and liqueurs. It has a higher concentration of menthol than other mint species and is therefore more highly prized by modern pharmacists as well as herbalists. The tea is used for nausea, indigestion, headaches, and as a cooling herb against fever.

Cautions

Peppermint is considered safe, even for ongoing daily use. My philosophy, however, is to drink no single herb habitually, in case your body finds it toxic in excess.

Botanical Notes

There are more than 30 species in the *Mentha* genus. Most mints are low-growing, invasive perennials. The tiny purple, pink, or white flowers are insignificant. The leaves are the valued part of the plant. Peppermint is easy to grow and a satisfying container plant for deck or patio.

Rosemary
ROSMARINUS OFFICINALIS

Flavor

Rosemary has a pinelike, resinous flavor, with a subtle sweetness in the aftertaste.

History and Folklore

✧ Legend has it that the flowers of the rosemary plant were originally white. When the Virgin Mary draped her blue cloak on a rosemary shrub during her escape with the Christ child from Herod's soldiers, the flowers turned

Smell it oft and it shall keep thee youngly.
—Banckes Herbal, 1525

from white to blue. Mary's Mantle is one of the plant's many colloquial names

✧ St. Thomas More said of rosemary: "I let it run all over my garden wall, not only because my bees love it, but because it is the herb sacred to remembrance, and therefore to friendship." In the lore of many civilizations, rosemary is mentioned as a memory-strengthening herb.

Modern Uses

Rosemary is thought to keep the hair shiny and is therefore added to many commercial hair preparations. It is also a component in many perfumes and potpourris and is a wonderful, bracing bath herb. Rosemary enjoys supreme status in the cuisines of the Mediterranean regions, where it thrives in the hot, arid climate.

Medicinally, rosemary is used as an overall tonic and is believed beneficial for the stomach and circulatory system. Headaches may also be helped by rosemary tea. Rosemary is listed as an official medicine in the U.S. Pharmacopoeia, but it is potentially quite toxic.

Cautions

In its pure and concentrated form, oil of rosemary is considered a stomach and kidney irritant, potentially a dangerous toxin. It is wise, therefore, to confine one's use of the tea to 1 cup per day.

Botanical Notes
Rosemary is a tender, evergreen perennial with needlelike leaves. It is slow-growing and bushy. The small flowers are usually pale blue or white in color and are suitable for teas, as are the leaves. The plant blooms in late spring in most climates. Rosemary can take the full intensity of the sun.

chapter
FOUR

TEATIME
TREATS

I find the British tradition of afternoon tea charming, convivial, and refreshing. Those of us who need a good pick-me-up around 4 o'clock daily, whatever our nationality, can begin a similar cozy tradition in our own parlors or kitchens or nooks. Even without the caffeine provided by a cup of strong Darjeeling or Oolong, the tea break cheers and rejuvenates, particularly when the brew is accompanied by a tray of delicious, sweet morsels.

The flavors and aromas of herbal teas are a perfect match for many of my favorite cookies and cakes. Teas that are pungent with ginger, cinnamon, fennel, or cloves taste just right with a spice-laced treat such as Fresh Ginger Cakes or Spiced Sesame Cakes. Tasty fruit-flavored cakes or cookies—such as Jam Thumbprints—become even more wonderful when served with herbal teas that exude the aromas of berries or apples. A citrus-scented tea is my favorite beverage with Orange Oatmeal Walnut Cookies or Lemon Pecan Biscotti. Two other long-cherished treats at my house, Honey Nut Bread and Buttermilk Poppyseed Scones, happily nestle up to any cup of herbal tea.

I suppose that none of these treats qualifies as health food, except perhaps for the soul. A couple of them are made without butter, however, so saturated fat and cholesterol are kept to a minimum.

For an easy, novel, and absolutely cozy social event, plan a tea party! Serve two or three special sweet treats, of various tastes and textures, with several of your favorite herbal tea blends. Offer caffeinated tea, as well, if you think some of your guests will want it. Place the table where there will be a view of the garden in spring or summer, or by a roaring fire in cold weather. Set it with your prettiest linens, china, and utensils. Put on a recording of uplifting classical music or light jazz.

When your guests arrive, put the kettle on to boil, and forget about the world for at least an hour or two. No serious talk at teatime, please!

Baking Tips for Beginners

Here are just a few short notes about baking, in general, for readers who may be unfamiliar with such things.

✧ Have all your ingredients at room temperature before making a recipe. This means refrigerated ingredients, such as butter and eggs, should be set out on the counter for an hour or two before mixing.

✧ Be sure to preheat the oven at least 10–15 minutes before beginning your recipe. Purchase an inexpensive oven thermometer and see how long your particular oven takes to

No sooner had the warm liquid, and the crumbs with it, touched my palate than a shudder ran through my whole body, and I stopped, intent upon the extraordinary changes that were taking place. An exquisite pleasure had invaded my senses . . .

—Marcel Proust

come up to temperature after the dial is set. After 20 minutes, if the temperature indicated on the dial is not accurately reflected by the thermometer, you may adjust the dial upward or downward to compensate. Be sure the oven is at the correct temperature before putting your cake or cookies in the oven.

✧ Some bakers swear that the sifting of flour is essential for good results. I am too impatient for this in the case of cookies and quick breads and achieve fine results without sifting.

✧ Unless otherwise indicated in a recipe, remove cookies to a rack or platter to cool in one layer. You may, of course, serve them warm. Allow any surviving cookies to cool completely before storing. Pack loosely in an airtight tin or a jar out of direct light, and store at room temperature. Most cookies will remain fresh for at least a week under these conditions.

Orange Walnut Oatmeal Cookies

I enjoy experimenting with flavor extracts, which provide a pleasant backdrop for other tastes when used sparingly. This combination of orange with cinnamon and walnuts is superb.

Unbleached all-purpose flour	1 cup
Baking powder	1 teaspoon
Ground cinnamon	1 teaspoon
Salt	A pinch
Light brown sugar, lightly packed	$^1/_2$ cup
Granulated sugar	$^1/_3$ cup
Butter, at room temperature	$^1/_2$ cup
Whole egg	1 large
Orange extract	1 teaspoon
Quick-cooking rolled oats	1 cup
Raw, unsalted walnuts, chopped	$^3/_4$ cup

Preheat the oven to 350° F. In a bowl, stir together the flour, baking powder, cinnamon, and salt. Set aside.

In a larger bowl, stir the sugars together, then cream with the butter until well combined. Add the egg and orange extract and beat until fluffy. Add the flour mixture and stir vigorously until incorporated. Stir in the oats and walnuts until well combined.

Drop by small spoonfuls onto an unoiled baking sheet, allowing 2 inches between cookies. Bake 15 minutes at 350° F.

Jam Thumbprints

These are festive cookies, with their crinkled tops, sugar sparkles, and colorful jam centers. Choose a jam made with fruits that complement the flavor of the tea you will serve with the cookies—raspberry jam with Very Berry Blend, for instance. If there are children about, let them help with the jam filling. They will consider it great fun and will enjoy the cookies all the more for having had a hand in making them.

YIELD: ABOUT 1 1/2 DOZEN

Unbleached all-purpose flour	1 1/4 cups
Baking powder	1 teaspoon
Salt	A pinch
Butter, at room temperature	1/2 cup
Light brown sugar, lightly packed	1/2 cup
Whole egg	1 large
Vanilla extract	1/2 teaspoon
Granulated sugar	1/4 cup
Jam of your choice	3 tablespoons

Preheat the oven to 375° F. In a bowl, stir together the flour, baking powder, and salt. Set aside.

In a larger bowl, cream the butter with the sugar until well combined. Add the egg and vanilla and beat until fluffy. Add the flour mixture and stir until well incorporated. Roll the dough into a large ball.

Place the granulated sugar in a shallow layer on a plate. With your hands, pinch off pieces of the dough and shape into 1-inch balls. Roll in the sugar to lightly coat them, then place them 2 inches apart on an unoiled baking sheet. Bake 5 minutes at 375° F. Remove the cookies from the oven and make a small indentation in the center of each one with your thumb or the back of a spoon. Return to the oven and bake 7–10 minutes longer, until lightly browned.

Remove the cookies from the oven, transfer them to a wire rack or platter to cool for a few minutes, then spoon 1/2 teaspoon of jam into each of the indentations. Serve while still slightly warm, if possible.

Should I, after tea and cakes and ices, have the strength to force the moment to its crisis?

—T.S. Eliot

Lemon Pecan Biscotti

There seems to be a mystique surrounding the making of biscotti, those irresistibly crunchy Italian dipping cookies that are the current rage. Actually, they are quick and simple to make, though they do spend more time in the oven than most cookies. I consider them fun because the dough loaves are shaped by hand, which harkens me back to my mud pie days. The lemon and pecan flavors combine well with any fruity or spicy tea. For another tasty version, try the aniseed and almond variation. And don't forget to dunk!

YIELD: ABOUT 3 DOZEN

Unbleached all-purpose flour	3 cups
Baking powder	2 teaspoons
Salt	A pinch
Whole eggs	2 large
Canola oil	3/4 cup
Granulated sugar	3/4 cup
Vanilla extract	1/2 teaspoon
Lemon extract	1 1/2 teaspoons
Raw, unsalted pecans, minced	1 cup

Preheat the oven to 350° F. In a bowl, stir together the flour, baking powder, and salt. Set aside.

In a larger bowl, combine the eggs, oil, sugar, and extracts and beat until well combined. Add the flour and pecans and stir until incorporated. The mixture will be very thick and sticky. Work it with your hands if the spoon seems too awkward, just until all the ingredients are well combined.

Divide the dough into thirds. Using your hands, place one third of the dough on a standard unoiled baking sheet and form into an elongated loaf about 1 inch thick and 3–4 inches wide. It should be of uniform shape and thickness for best results. Flatten the ends of the loaf by pressing in on them with the palm of your hand.

Arrange the first loaf at an angle on one end of the sheet, then proceed with the remaining two portions of dough. The loaves should not touch on the sheet, but they can be arranged close together.

Bake for 25 minutes at 350° F. Remove the pan from the oven and use a sharp knife to cut the loaves into $1/2$-inch slices. Lay the slices down on one side and return to the oven. Bake 5 minutes, remove the pan, and turn the slices over. Bake an additional 5 minutes. Cool the biscotti on the pan.

Biscotti are delicious warm from the oven, and they improve over time! They can be stored for many weeks in an airtight container at room temperature. As they age, they will become more dry and crisp.

Aniseed and Almond Variation: Omit the lemon extract. Increase the vanilla extract to 1 teaspoon and add $1/2$ teaspoon almond extract. Omit the pecans, adding $1 1/2$ tablespoons lightly crushed aniseed to the batter in their place.

Fresh Ginger Cakes

This is a not-quite-classic version because fresh ginger root is used instead of the dried powder. These cookies have a rich brown color that is nicely highlighted by powdered sugar if you don't mind the extra step. I like this cookie with citrus-flavored teas as well as those made from aromatic spices.

Unbleached all-purpose flour	2 cups
Baking powder	2 teaspoons
Allspice	1 1/2 teaspoons
Salt	1/8 teaspoon
Butter, at room temperature	6 tablespoons
Dark brown sugar, lightly packed	3/4 cup
Whole eggs	2 large
Molasses	1/4 cup
Coffee, brewed strong	2 tablespoons
Grated fresh ginger root	1 1/2 tablespoons
Powdered sugar	(optional)

Preheat the oven to 325° F. Lightly oil a baking sheet and set aside.

In a bowl, stir together the flour, baking powder, allspice, and salt. Set aside.

In a larger bowl, cream the butter with the sugar until well combined. Add the eggs, molasses, coffee, and ginger and beat until fluffy. Add the flour mixture and stir vigorously until incorporated.

Lightly oil your hands. Roll the dough into 1-inch balls and place them 2 inches apart on the oiled baking sheet. Bake

15 minutes at 325° F. Allow to cool for a few minutes, then dust the tops lightly with powdered sugar shaken through a wire mesh strainer, if you wish.

Spiced Sesame Cakes

These cake-like cookies have an exotic aroma and are light, almost fluffy, in texture. Toasting sesame seeds brings out their nuttiness; however, some may prefer the flavor untoasted. Enjoy these tantalizing little cakes with any tea that has a hint of spice or with a simple cup of chamomile.

YIELD: ABOUT 1 1/2 DOZEN

Sesame seeds	2 tablespoons
Whole wheat pastry flour	1 1/2 cups
Ground cardamom	2 teaspoons
Baking powder	1 teaspoon
Ground cinnamon	1/2 teaspoon
Ground cloves	1/4 teaspoon
Salt	A pinch
Pepper	Several grinds
Whole eggs	2 large
Honey, warmed	1/3 cup
Tahini (sesame butter)	1/4 cup
Maple syrup	2 tablespoons
Lemon extract	1 teaspoon

Preheat the oven to 350° F. Lightly oil a baking sheet and set aside. Place the sesame seeds in a dry, heavy-bottomed skillet over medium heat. When they barely begin to color, shake the pan around on the burner so seeds brown evenly. When lightly browned, remove the seeds to a small bowl or plate and set aside.

In a small bowl, stir together the flour, cardamom, baking powder, cinnamon, cloves, salt, and pepper. Stir in most of the toasted sesame seeds, reserving about 1 teaspoon. In a large bowl, beat together the eggs, honey, tahini, syrup, and lemon extract until well combined. Add the flour mixture and stir until all ingredients are smoothly incorporated.

Drop by the spoonful onto the oiled baking sheet. Top each cookie with a few of the reserved sesame seeds. Bake for 12 minutes at 350° F, then allow to cool on the pan for 10 minutes before serving or storing.

Buttermilk Poppyseed Scones

I love scones in all their variations. This version enlivens a basic batter with the tang of buttermilk and the crunch of poppyseeds. For an extra special treat, split the scones in half after baking and serve them warm with jam and crème fraîche or what in England is called Devonshire cream. Good old American sour cream with a couple of tablespoons of unwhipped heavy cream stirred in would be an acceptable substitute.

Unbleached all-purpose flour	1 1/2 cups
Whole wheat pastry flour	1 1/2 cups
Poppy seeds	3 tablespoons
Baking powder	1 tablespoon
Salt	1/4 teaspoon
Buttermilk	1 cup
Honey, warmed	1/3 cup
Orange juice or water	2 tablespoons
Butter, melted	1/3 cup

Preheat the oven to 350° F. Lightly oil a baking sheet and set aside. In a bowl, stir together the flours, poppy seeds, baking powder, and salt. Set aside.

In a larger bowl, beat the buttermilk, honey, and orange juice or water together until well blended. Add half the flour mixture and beat until incorporated, then add the melted butter a little at a time, beating well after each addition. Stir in the remaining flour mixture, just until incorporated, and turn out onto a floured work surface.

Turn and knead the dough several strokes, then divide into thirds and form each third into a uniform circular loaf. Cut each loaf into quarters and place the wedges on the baking sheet. Bake about 20 minutes at 350° F, until lightly browned.

Honey Nut Bread

A form of this rich and delicious quick bread first appeared in a cookbook entitled Fast and Natural Cuisine, *my first collaboration with good friend Susann Geiskopf-Hadler. It was published in 1983. To my delight, the recipes and the partnership have stood the test of time.*

YIELD: 1 LOAF

Whole wheat pastry flour	1 cup
Unbleached all-purpose flour	1 cup
Baking powder	1 1/2 teaspoons
Salt	1/2 teaspoon
Whole eggs	2 large
Honey, warmed	1/2 cup
Butter, melted	2 tablespoons
Buttermilk	3/4 cup
Raw, unsalted walnuts or pecans, chopped	1 cup
Golden raisins	1/3 cup
Nutmeg, grated	1/4 teaspoon

Preheat the oven to 325° F. Butter the bottom and sides of a standard loaf pan and set aside in a cool place.

In a bowl, stir together the flours, baking powder, and salt. Set aside.

In a larger bowl, beat the eggs for a minute, then add the honey and butter and beat until well combined. Beat in the buttermilk. Add the flour mixture and mix well, then fold in the nuts and raisins.

Pour the batter into the buttered loaf pan and dust the top with nutmeg, preferably freshly grated. Bake 50–60 minutes at 325° F, until nicely browned and a toothpick inserted in the center comes out clean. Cool in the pan for 10 minutes, then transfer to a wire rack or bread board to finish cooling.

Among the body's remedies
are none more wondrous than herb teas.
These gifts of Nature's widsom used
to strengthen, purify, and soothe
do offer pleasure as they heal.
Thus do the herbs God's hand reveal.
—Dame Margaret Perry Woodson

chapter
FIVE

HERBAL TEAS AS GENTLE MEDICINES

H erbal medicine is an ancient and well-documented art. There is archeological evidence that humans in Mesopotamia utilized herbs for healing some 6,000 years ago. The earliest known Chinese herbal dates from about 2,700 B.C., though references to herbal healing in China go back much further than that. The ancient Egyptians used plants as medicine, as well as an ingredient in cosmetics, perfumes, and food seasonings. The Old Testament mentions the use of herbs to treat disease.

The East Indian healing philosophy called Ayurveda ("science of life") has employed herbs for thousands of years and significantly influenced the development of the herbalists's art throughout the world. Some Ayurvedic medical volumes are nearly 3,500 years old and are still used as official textbooks.

The first European treatise on the use of herbs, *De Materia Medica,* was compiled by Greek physician Dioscorides in the first century A.D. Here in America, native peoples have long known and used the power of plants for healing—and passed on some of their wisdom to the pioneers.

Before this century—during which the science and business of pharmacology have become well established—people around the world depended on herbs for their medicines. The person who possessed the greatest skill in identifying herbs and putting them to use as curatives was among the most highly regarded residents of a village or region.

The herbalist of old made and used plant extracts, tinctures, oils, ointments, and poultices, as well as simple teas. She was the predecessor of today's physician, and the humble plants she utilized for healing became the sources for some of today's most highly valued pharmaceuticals. Digitalis, used to regulate heartbeat in people with arrhythmia, is derived from foxglove. Aspirin contains substances originally synthesized from the bark of the white willow tree. Ephedrine and pseudoephedrine—contained in many over-the-counter cold remedies—are derived from ephedra, a plant used in China to treat colds and flus for more than 5,000 years.

Today we have available for our use a vast array of synthesized drugs and a tremendous army of doctors to prescribe them. Of course, we are grateful for the availability of potent pharmaceuticals when we are seriously ill and in need of fast and sure relief from symptoms. The science of pharmacology has delivered cures for many ailments which, in ages past, were commonly fatal. Drugs provide precise quantities of specific substances and are therefore easy to study, prescribe, and use. But pharmaceuticals are not without their dangers. Almost every pill or potion available at the local drugstore is packaged with a long list of potential side effects.

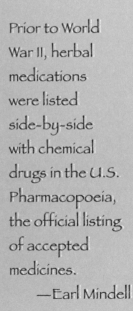

Prior to World War II, herbal medications were listed side-by-side with chemical drugs in the U.S. Pharmacopoeia, the official listing of accepted medicines.

—Earl Mindell

So the simple and natural appeal of herbs endures. There are times when we experience mild symptoms and desire a mild remedy, one with gentle action and no known side effects. This is when herbal teas, such as those recommended in this book, can satisfy our needs.

Remember that the herbs are part of nature's plan for our healing; they tone and balance our entire system. Some teas do offer immediate relief from symptoms, but dramatic cures are not always part of the picture. When using medicinal teas for acute illness, keep up the treatment for 2–3 days and trust the process.

A Cautionary Note

As discussed above, herbs have been used for healing in every age and throughout the world. They do not, however, enjoy the approval of the modern medical establishment, often due to the fact that they have not been adequately studied in state-of-the-art laboratories. Modern medicine is built on scientific evidence that can be measured and reproduced. Much of herbal medicine is based on experiential evidence—the carefully recorded observations of learned herbalists and the testimony of those who have received herbal treatments.

The debate about the efficacy and safety of herbs as medicines is not likely to be resolved anytime soon. Both camps feel certain of their positions. I maintain that the only meaningful approach to the question is to experiment cautiously on one's own, as many herbal proponents have done. Personal experience often convinces us that benefit can be derived from the careful use of certain herbs when we are faced with minor illness. The key word here is *careful*. Herbs, as well as drugs, must be used with respect.

When it comes to herbal teas, responsibility for healing rests in our own hands. There is wonderful freedom in this, but please exercise awareness and caution, and don't hesitate to consult a physician if your symptoms persist or worsen.

To minimize the risk of adverse effects, I recommend against habitual, long-term use of any single medicinal herb. With herbal teas—as with all foods and beverages—moderation is the essence of wisdom.

Also, be sure of your sources. When dried, many plants look alike and are easily confused by the amateur. If you grow and dry your own, you can be certain of the source and purity of the herbs in your cupboard. This is often not possible, however, so seek out a local herb supplier and learn how they control the quality of their products. If there are no herbalists in

The path of the herbalist is to open ourselves to nature in an innocent and pure way. She in turn will open her bounty and reward us with her many valuable secrets.

—Michael Tierra

your region, consult the mail-order resources at the back of this book (page 116).

Pregnant and lactating women should be especially careful. It is best at these times to avoid heavy or prolonged use of any herb without proper guidance. Consult a qualified herbal practitioner if you wish to include herbs in your pregnancy self-care program.

People with severe allergies to certain plants, the elderly, and the very young are also advised to minimize their use of medicinal herbs unless under professional care.

These precautions duly delivered, I advise you to relax and enjoy. The teas recommended in this book are made from well-known plants considered safe and widely recommended by respected modern herbalists. You may use them with ease and confidence.

> The fundamental principle of true healing consists of a return to natural habits of living.
>
> —Jethro Kloss

A NOTE ABOUT THE REMEDIES

There is always a vast number of herbs to choose from that can be helpful in treating any single condition. Herbalists take many variables into consideration when designing individual herbal treatments. The remedies discussed in the sections that follow are not the only herbal teas that might help your condition, nor are they offered as miracle cures.

In choosing the teas to recommend for each ailment, I have been careful to avoid those herbs considered potentially dangerous for significant numbers of people. My intention is to suggest effective herbal tea remedies that can be used safely without expert supervision. These suggestions combine the knowledge of many skilled herbalists with that gleaned from my own use of medicinal teas over two decades' time.

Because the medicine in plants is powerful, it is important to not overdo their use. One or two cups of any particular tea per day, unless otherwise indicated, is enough to have a beneficial effect.

I hope you will find, as I have, that these simple beverages—used wisely—help restore you to ease and a greater sense of overall health and well-being.

ASTHMA/BRONCHITIS

Asthma is an upper-respiratory ailment resulting from an allergic reaction to pollens, dust, animal dander, molds, or other airborne irritants. Asthma is potentially serious and can even be fatal if not treated. Consult a physician when wheezing is severe and/or breathing is difficult or painful.

Part of the cure for asthma, naturally, is to avoid the irritating substances as much as possible. Dietary changes may also help—such foods as milk, eggs, nuts, and seafood have been known to trigger asthma reactions.

The upper-respiratory infection called bronchitis is typically viral in nature and therefore impervious to antibiotics. A bacterial type of bronchitis does occur, however, so consult a doctor to determine the best course of treatment if you have a severe and sustained cough. An acute case of bronchitis will usually run its course in one to two weeks. Chronic bronchitis can last for months.

There are some time-tested herbs that can help alleviate the symptoms of upper-respiratory illness and aid the healing process.

Mullein and Anise Blend

Here is a mild and pleasant tea for phlegmy bronchial conditions.

1 1/2 cups water
1 teaspoon dried aniseed
1 teaspoon dried mullein leaves

Bring water to a boil in a glass or stainless steel pan. Add the aniseed, reduce heat to medium-high, and simmer, uncovered, 5 minutes. Meanwhile, place the mullein in a teapot. Without straining, pour the anise decoction over the mullein leaves, cover, and steep 10 minutes. Strain, sweeten with honey, and sip slowly while warm.

Thyme, Cayenne, and Peppermint

This somewhat stimulating blend is good for times when we want relief from our bronchial symptoms but can't simply stay home and rest. Carry the warm tea in a thermos to the office and sip in 1/2-cup doses a few times throughout the day.

1 tablespoon dried peppermint
2 teaspoons dried thyme
1/8 teaspoon cayenne pepper
2 cups water, barely boiled

Place the herbs in a teapot. Pour the boiling water over them, cover, and steep 5 minutes. Strain and sweeten with honey. Sip slowly while still warm.

In the Middle Ages, a popular remedy for melancholy was to sleep on a pillow stuffed with thyme, which was though to lift and invigorate the spirits.

BLADDER INFECTIONS

Any woman who has suffered bladder infections knows true misery. She feels relentless pressure on the bladder without being able to urinate and an intense burning sensation when urine is passed. Fortunately, relief is available, though it can never arrive soon enough!

Bladder infections are typically caused by infection with *E. coli,* a common bacteria. When *E. coli* invades the urethra and bladder, a painful infection can result.

When infection does occur, begin to fight it immediately by drinking copious quantities of water, which will help flush bacteria out of the bladder. Drinking cranberry juice is a popular folk remedy for bladder infections, and recent studies suggest the sour juice does have an antiseptic effect in the urinary tract. Since it might help, and can't hurt, you may wish to include unsweetened cranberry juice in your fluid therapy.

A doctor can run tests to confirm the source of your infection and will prescribe antibiotics that are effective in eliminating the culprit. Meanwhile, aspirin and ibuprofen have anti-inflammatory properties and can therefore reduce the burn of a bladder infection. Do not exceed recommended dosage, no matter how severe your symptoms.

Warm baths can be soothing while you wait out the cure, as can the following herbal beverages.

Bladder Blend

Arctostaphylos uva ursi *is also known as bearberry. It has long been favored by herbalists as a cystitis remedy. Yarrow provides mild anesthetic action, and thyme is an anti-inflammatory.*

1 teaspoon dried corn silk
1 teaspoon dried uva ursi leaves
1 teaspoon dried yarrow leaves
1/2 teaspoon dried thyme leaves
1/2 teaspoon dried marshmallow root
1 cup water, barely boiled

Place the herbs in a teapot and pour the boiling water over them. Cover and steep for 10 minutes. Sweeten with honey, if desired. Sip slowly in 1/2-cup doses throughout the day.

Celery Seed, Alfalfa, and Garlic

Be sure to purchase celery seed at a grocery store or herb shop rather than a nursery. The seed sold for the garden may be treated with unwanted chemicals. Celery tea can help induce urination. It is not recommended for serious kidney ailments or for pregnant women.

1 1/2 cups water
1/4 teaspoon celery seed
1 teaspoon dried alfalfa
1 clove garlic, minced

Bring water to a boil in a glass or stainless steel pan. Add the celery seed and reduce heat to medium-high. Simmer, uncovered, 5 minutes. Meanwhile, place the alfalfa and garlic in the teapot. Pour the unstrained celery seed decoction into the pot, cover, and steep for 5 minutes. Strain, sweeten with honey, and sip slowly while warm.

COLDS AND FLU

It is no accident that the basic runny-nose, sore-throat, fever-and-cough condition is called a *common* cold—everyone gets one now and then. Likewise, most people have been laid low by a flu bug at least once or twice. In fact, colds and flu are among our most frequent physical maladies, and they can make us miserable.

Since it is viruses that are responsible for flu illness and for the common cold, antibiotics are no help in our recovery. Over-the-counter medications become most people's only comfort until the illness runs its course. There are safe and simple home remedies, however, that can offer relief.

Staying warm is critical, since the immune system will utilize whatever resources are necessary to maintain the body's temperature. This detracts from important disease-fighting processes. So dress warmly and use plenty of blankets on the bed to keep your temperature up.

Many people—plenty of doctors among them—swear that vitamin C helps prevent colds and flu, and that it is an effective treatment as well. Since there is no known risk involved in moderate vitamin C therapy, it may be wise to take 2–3 grams a day throughout your illness, starting when your symptoms first appear. Take a time-release tablet, or a few 500 mg tablets per day, rather than one large dose all at once. You may want to continue taking vitamin C daily after you are well to test its effectiveness as a preventative.

Saltwater gargles can be used as often as needed to soothe a sore throat (remember to spit the water out after gargling; don't swallow it). The section on Sore Throats/Hoarseness (page 99) offers further suggestions for smoothing out a scratchy throat. Also see the section on Coughs (page 77).

If you have a long-lasting high fever, wheezing (whistling in the lungs), or intense aching or swelling in the ears, sinuses, lungs, or glands, see a doctor for a thorough evaluation of your condition. Meanwhile, refrain from smoking, eat healthy foods, rest, and drink plenty of fluids, including the following teas.

Hot Ginger Lemonade

This is the old standby remedy in my home for any cold or flu-like illness. We also drink it when we are healthy but our friends are ill, to help keep our immune systems strong. The tea tastes good, the steam from the cup clears congestion, and the overall effect is extremely relaxing. You may add an ounce of brandy to your bedtime dose to help ease you into slumber.

An ounce of prevention is worth a pound of cure.

—Benjamin Franklin

1 1/2 cups water
3 1/4-inch slices fresh ginger root, bruised
1/2 of a fresh lemon
1 teaspoon honey
1/4 teaspoon powdered cayenne pepper

Bring water to a boil in a glass or stainless steel pan. Meanwhile, cut 3 1/4-inch slices from a piece of fresh ginger root and hit each slice gently with the broad side of a knife to break up the pulp a bit. Put the ginger in the boiling water and simmer uncovered 5 minutes. Meanwhile, squeeze the juice from the lemon into a cup. Add the honey and cayenne. Strain the ginger tea into the cup, stir, and sip slowly while hot.

Cooling Blend

Rose hips deliver a large dose of vitamin C, while peppermint and sage both have a cooling effect on the system. This tea is particularly helpful with feverish colds. And it tastes good!

1 teaspoon crushed dried rose hips
1 teaspoon dried peppermint leaves
1 teaspoon dried sage leaves
1 cup water, barely boiled

Place the herbs in a teapot. Pour the boiling water over the herbs, cover, and steep 10 minutes. Strain and sweeten with honey to taste. Sip slowly while warm.

COUGHS

Coughs are among the most miserable facts of life. They disturb the peace in many ways, disrupting our sleep and depleting our energy. Our lungs feel weak and sore, and we are powerless to control the tickling and hacking. Even cough drops and syrups offer only very temporary relief.

A cough can be a symptom of bronchitis or asthma. If you suspect either of these conditions, consult a physician to be advised of all treatment options (also, read the Asthma/Bronchitis section, page 69). For most of us, a cough is part of the bundle of symptoms that comes with a flu or cold.

Whatever its cause, an upper-respiratory ailment can be improved by refraining from smoking, drinking plenty of fluids, using chest rubs or poultices containing camphor, and inhaling steam (see directions under Sore Throats/Hoarseness, page 99). The following herbal teas can also offer relief.

Thyme, Hyssop, and Sage

This tea combines three age-old cough and congestion remedies. They are powerful medicines so should not be used excessively, but can be a godsend in small doses over the course of a few days. The tea can be gargled an ounce at a time for topical relief of a scratchy throat. For sipping, combine with plenty of honey for its throat-coating action.

For a cold in ye head, take sage leaves, rub them will, and apply them to ye nostrils in ye morning.
—from a 1650 pharmacist's book

1 teaspoon dried thyme
1 teaspoon dried hyssop
1 teaspoon dried sage leaves
1 cup water, barely boiled

Place the herbs in a teapot. Pour the boiling water over them, cover, and steep 10 minutes. Strain and sweeten with honey. Cool a bit and sip slowly in 1-ounce doses as needed (up to 2 cups a day for no more than a few successive days).

Linden and Licorice

This wonderful tasting tea is also good lung medicine. It can be drunk as often as desired during the course of a respiratory illness. (Licorice tea is not recommended for people prone to high blood pressure, pregnant women, or women with fibroids.)

1 1/2 cups water
1/4 teaspoon chopped dried licorice root
2 teaspoons dried linden flowers

Bring water to a boil in a glass or stainless steel pan. Add the licorice root, reduce heat to medium-high, and simmer 5 minutes. Meanwhile, place the linden flowers in a teapot. Pour the unstrained licorice decoction over the linden, cover, and steep 10 minutes. Sweeten with honey, if desired. Take in 1/2-cup doses, as needed.

FATIGUE

An occasional day of lethargy, sluggishness, depression, or general tiredness is quite common and easily remedied by waiting it out and getting a good night's sleep. A chronic lack of energy, however, can have a devastating impact on one's life.

In many cases, ongoing fatigue is a sign that we are working too hard, pushing ourselves relentlessly, and not honoring our bodies with proper nutrition, exercise, and rest.

Since our bodies use food to create energy, a balanced diet is an important contributor to a life of vitality. Such a diet combines proteins, carbohydrates, and fats in sensible proportions for optimal energy production. In general, complex carbohydrates are the longest-burning fuel for the body. Starting the day with a high-carbohydrate, low-fat meal can help prevent fatigue later in the day. A whole-grain, low-fat cereal, or a large bowl of fresh fruit, are both excellent choices for breakfast.

It may seem paradoxical, but giving the body a good physical workout tends to invigorate rather than deplete us. The notion that regular exercise increases energy is supported by a number of modern studies. It takes energy to make energy. Get up and move!

Not surprisingly, sleeping more is an important fatigue reliever for many people. Different people have different sleep requirements, but we all know when we're not getting enough. Make whatever adjustments are necessary to give yourself enough sleep time. You will be rewarded with a sharper mind as well as greater physical vitality.

Cold water is a tried-and-true energizer when we slip into listlessness or become sleepy while working. Splashing cold water on the face and running it over the hands can help considerably. (Even better is a cold shower or quick dip in an unheated pool, though these options are obviously not available to most people at the workplace.)

Another tip: Use work breaks for a walk outside or gentle stretching exercises, not for smoking cigarettes or drinking coffee. Such stimulants may provide an immediate lift but backfire over the course of a day as they overtax the body's metabolism. Instead of coffee or black tea, try these herbal teas whenever you want a pick-me-up.

Fennel and Rosemary

Here is a mildly stimulating tea, useful in increasing mental alertness. If you have fresh rosemary in your garden, you may substitute 1 tablespoon bruised fresh rosemary leaves for the dried amount specified below.

1 1/2 cups water
1/2 teaspoon fennel seed, crushed
1 teaspoon dried rosemary leaves

Bring water to a boil. Add the fennel seed, reduce heat to medium, and simmer 10 minutes. Pour the hot fennel water over the rosemary leaves, cover, and steep 5 minutes. Strain and sweeten with honey, if desired. Allow to cool a bit and sip slowly while warm.

Garlic Cocktail

This is a wonderful all-purpose tonic, good for boosting immune function as well as our energy level.

1 cup water, barely boiled
1 large clove garlic
2 tablespoons fresh lemon juice
1 teaspoon honey
A pinch cayenne

Combine all ingredients in a cup and pour boiling water over the mixture. Stir to dissolve the honey and allow to steep 5 minutes. Do not strain. Sip while warm.

Ginseng Brew

For thousands of years, the Chinese have sworn by the stimulating effect of ginseng. However, it is not recommended for pregnant or lactating women or anyone with an inflammatory or feverish condition. Carefully check your source, as ginseng is a profitable trade and is therefore subject to fraudulent labeling. Use Korean or Chinese ginseng (Panax ginseng) or Siberian ginseng (Eleutherococus senticosus) for best results.

A pinch of ginseng
1 cup water, barely boiled

Place the ginseng in a cup. Pour the boiling water over it and steep 5 minutes. Sip slowly while warm.

FEVER

Any illness involving infection by a virus or bacteria can involve fever, since intense heat is one of the body's defenses against the invading organism. Fevers should be perceived as a sign that the immune system is doing its job properly. Too high a temperature or one sustained for too long can harm the system, however, and should be treated.

Any illness that includes high or long-lasting fevers should be evaluated by a doctor. However, there are home remedies that may be employed to good effect.

Perhaps the most important part of fever therapy is to drink plenty of fluids. Since fever causes perspiration, it is a dehydrating condition. Replacing fluids helps to keep the temperature-regulating mechanism functioning properly and also helps to flush out bacteria through the urine and mucous. Avoid cold, sugary, or alcoholic beverages. Instead drink plenty of room-temperature spring water and fresh fruit and vegetable juices. Cool (not ice-cold) lemonade made with spring water and fresh lemon juice and sweetened with honey is a terrific healing beverage and can be sipped as often as desired.

Despite the feeling of being overheated, don't strip to your underwear or throw off all the covers at night. This may bring on chills as the body's beleaguered immune systems deals with conflicting messages. If your fever does bring on the shivers, relax in a very warm, but not steaming hot, bath and then bundle up in bed.

Sponge baths with lukewarm water can help soothe a child's feverish state. Have the child drink plenty of cool spring water along with diluted freshly squeezed orange juice.

There is no consensus among the researchers about the "feed versus starve" question. If you feel hungry while you have a fever, eat fresh fruits and vegetables and whole grains, not processed foods or overly sweet or salty snacks. If you don't feel like eating, that's fine, too. But don't neglect the fluids, since they are essential to the healing process.

These teas can be a part of your fluid therapy when dealing with fever.

Sage and Peppermint
Fever was one of many conditions that certain Native American tribes treated with sage. The peppermint has an overall cooling influence.

If any man can name . . . all the properties of mint, he must know how many fish swim in the Indian Ocean.
—Wilafried of Strabo, 12th century

2 teaspoons dried sage
1 teaspoon dried peppermint
1 cup water, barely boiled

Place the herbs in a teapot. Pour the boiling water over them, cover, and steep 15 minutes. Strain and sweeten with honey, if desired. Sip slowly while warm, up to 3 cups a day.

Fenugreek, Thyme, and Cayenne
Three ancient herbs combine in this gentle fever remedy.

1 1/2 cups water
1 teaspoon dried fenugreek seeds
1 teaspoon dried thyme
1/4 teaspoon powered cayenne

Bring the water to a boil in a glass or stainless steel pan. Add the fenugreek seeds, reduce heat to medium-high, and simmer 5 minutes. Meanwhile, place the thyme in a teapot. Pour the unstrained fenugreek decoction over the thyme, cover, and steep 10 minutes. Strain, stir in the cayenne, and sweeten with honey, if desired. Sip slowly while warm.

HEADACHES
There is a long list of possible causes for headaches. Some of the frequently cited culprits are generalized tension, indiges-

tion, sinus pressure, hangover, caffeine withdrawal, allergic reactions, spinal misalignment, and dental problems. Cluster
headaches and the dreaded migraine, which may be hormonal
or genetic in nature, are in categories all their own.

Fortunately, many self-care techniques can be employed to
ward off headaches or minimize their impact once they've arrived. Since headaches are related to stress in many people, all
relaxation techniques—such as deep breathing and gentle
stretching—can help. A warm bath is another soothing therapy. Wet compresses applied to the head or neck are used to
good effect by many headache sufferers—some prefer them
very hot, others cold.

In the herb realm, lavender has long been used to alleviate
headaches. Its aroma, in particular, is considered beneficial.
Lavender oil is often recommended to people prone to mi-
graines as a massage oil for the temples. A handful of the dried
flowers or several drops of lavender oil added to very hot water
in a basin makes a wonderful "tea" for soaking the feet. The
fragrance of the lavender is soothing, and the heat of the water
will draw blood to the lower extremities, perhaps helping to
relieve the throbbing in your head.

If you suspect food allergies may be causing your
headaches, avoid this list of frequently implicated foods:
monosodium glutamate (MSG), artificial sweeteners and other

synthetic flavoring agents and preservatives, nuts, dairy products, salt, and chocolate. A professional allergist may be able to help you pinpoint your problem, or you may follow the rotation diet described in many holistic health handbooks to discover for yourself which foods are responsible.

Just as the cause of a headache may be difficult to pinpoint, so is the corresponding cure. Effective remedies seem to vary from person so person, so experimentation is recommended. Modern herbalists generally agree that certain herbs can be helpful to many people. The teas discussed below are all quite pleasant and safe. Drink up to 3 cups a day, as needed.

Scarborough Fair Blend

If you have an herb garden, these three culinary classics are probably growing outside your door. If this is the case, substitute 1 teaspoon each of bruised fresh leaves for the dried amounts given below.

1/2 teaspoon dried sage
1/2 teaspoon rosemary
1/2 teaspoon thyme leaves
1 cup water, barely boiled

Place the herbs in a teapot. Pour the boiling water over them, cover, and steep 10 minutes. Strain and sweeten with honey, if desired. Sip while warm.

Lemon Balm and Lavender

Lemon balm is so easy to grow, I almost always have fresh leaves on hand. When fresh is not available, you may substitute 1 teaspoon dried leaves, though the active medicinal properties are considered far superior in the fresh plant.

1 tablespoon chopped fresh lemon balm leaves
1 teaspoon dried lavender flowers
1 cup water, barely boiled

Place the herbs in a teapot. Pour the boiling water over them, cover, and steep 10 minutes. Strain, sweeten with honey, if desired, and sip while warm.

INDIGESTION

Another complaint commonplace enough to be considered a plague is indigestion. It takes many distressing forms. Gas and bloating, stomach cramps, and heartburn are variations on the same theme—you have eaten something that doesn't agree with you. It seems obvious but bears restating: If you are troubled by indigestion, you need to pay attention to what—and how—you are eating.

Certain people simply can't handle certain foods. Rich or greasy foods, onions and garlic, cruciferous vegetables, spicy foods, milk, and beans are common culprits. Poor food combining is another frequently cited cause of poor digestion, and food allergies are a reality for many people.

Without making any drastic changes in your diet, keep a food diary for a couple of weeks to find any patterns that may occur in your digestive upsets. This can help you determine which foods or combinations of foods are the troublemakers. Then follow through by making the necessary changes, even if it means giving up a cherished combination like hotdogs and beer.

Poor eating habits are often to blame for poor digestion. Eating too fast, eating too much, not chewing adequately, and gulping air when we swallow are some of the ways we bring indigestion upon ourselves. Many natural health practitioners suggest that drinking beverages with meals may cause indigestion. Fluids dilute intestinal juices that work best at full strength. Cold beverages may be especially detrimental, since they cool down the stomach. A certain level of heat is required for good digestion.

Sometimes, chronic indigestion is a symptom of a more serious ailment, such as an ulcer. If you have ongoing severe digestive upsets, consult a physician just to rule out any major problems.

While you are in the process of overhauling your eating habits and investigating the possibility of food allergies, try one of the following teas for relief of symptoms.

The Ginger Cure

Ginger has been used for centuries as a cure for flatulence and stomach cramping. Here it is combined with fennel and basil for an effective and quite pleasant brew. You are likely to enjoy immediate relief upon sipping a cup—no gulping or you may worsen your problem!

1 1/2 cups water, barely boiled
1 ounce fresh ginger root, thinly sliced and bruised
1/2 teaspoon dried fennel seed, crushed
1 teaspoon dried basil leaves

Bring water to a boil in a glass or stainless steel pan. Meanwhile, cut the ginger into 1/4-inch slices and hit each slice gently with the broad side of a knife to break up the pulp a little. Place the ginger in a teapot, along with the fennel seed and basil. Pour the boiling water over the herbs, cover, and steep 10 minutes. Strain and sweeten with honey if desired. Sip slowly while warm.

Peppermint Power

Here is another good therapy for digestive distress. Fenugreek is an ancient healing herb indigenous to India but widely available in the U.S. for culinary as well as medicinal purposes. The combination with peppermint happens to be tasty as well as effective, especially against stomach cramps.

1 cup water
1 teaspoon dried fenugreek seeds
1 teaspoon dried peppermint leaves

Bring water to a boil in a glass or stainless steel pan. Add the fenugreek seeds, reduce heat to medium-high, and simmer 5 minutes. Meanwhile, place the peppermint in a teapot. Add the unstrained fenugreek decoction, cover, and steep 5 minutes. Strain and sweeten with honey, if desired. Sip slowly while warm.

INSOMNIA

Insomnia, the inability to sleep, is a plague of the modern world. When we spend our days in a continuous round of appointments, responsibilities, and duties—often depending on coffee or other stimulating beverages to hurry us through it all—it can be difficult to shut off the speed switch at bedtime and relax into sleep.

Simply slowing down during the day as much as possible, and avoiding or minimizing stimulants in the diet, can greatly help the insomniac. The use of relaxation techniques such as deep breathing, gentle stretching, and self-massage before bed can also be wonderful sleep aids.

Those who lead sedentary lives will find that regular vigorous exercise is a healthy outlet for the body's natural energy supply. After a day of physical exertion, the body will crave its rest at bedtime.

Quiet time before bed is another effective sleep enhancer. Don't watch television or listen to loud music right up until bedtime. Allow some time to simply sit in the quiet, listen to peaceful music, or do some light reading until you feel sleepy.

These lifestyle changes will bring great improvement to those who suffer from chronic sleeplessness. But there may still be occasions when overexcitement, mental turbulence, or excessive exhaustion make falling asleep difficult. At such times, try the following herb teas for a mild sedative effect. Some herbalists suggest that honey always be used to sweeten teas drunk at bedtime. Honey, they tell us, helps the body retain fluids, so you won't be awakened in the night by call of nature.

Field of Dreams

This recipe makes two cups of relaxing tea. Share with a friend, or refrigerate the remainder in a closed container and reheat gently the next night.

2 teaspoons dried chamomile flowers
2 teaspoons dried lavender flowers
2 teaspoons dried catnip leaves
2 cups water, barely boiled

Place the herbs in a teapot. Pour the boiling water over them, cover, and steep 10 minutes. Strain and sweeten with honey, if desired. Sip slowly while still hot, just before bed.

Those herbal teas which the French people call tisanes . . . are simply hot water poured over a few dried leaves of mint or verbena or lime flowers or chamomile. They smooth out wrinkles in your mind miraculously, and make you sleep, with sweet dreams, too.

—M.F.K. Fisher

91

Peppermint Milk

In my rural area, organic milk has become available. It does not contain the traces of antibiotics and hormones present in most milk produced for the market. Seek out an organic brand, if you can, and avoid unnecessary chemical components.

1 heaping tablespoon peppermint leaves
1 cup organic lowfat milk

Heat the milk just to the boiling point. Pour it over the peppermint, cover, and steep 10 minutes. Strain and sweeten with honey, if desired. Sip slowly while hot.

MENOPAUSE

The "change of life" is dreaded by some women, perhaps because they associate it with the aging process and mourn the passing of their childbearing years. Others, however, celebrate the time as a transition into maturity when children are grown and more time is available for personal pursuits, wisdom blossoms, and sexuality is liberated from birth control concerns. Attitude is certainly a key factor in the experience of menopause.

However positive our attitude may be, menopause is often accompanied by distressing physical symptoms we would rather do without. Hot flashes, night sweats, vaginal dryness, mood swings, etc.—all associated with the diminishing flow of estrogen—can be treated. Estrogen replacement therapy is used by some women to regulate the hormonal flow. There are risks associated with this therapy, however, that we should learn about so we can make an informed decision. A discussion with a progressive-thinking doctor (preferably a woman who has passed menopause herself) can acquaint you with your options and help you decide on a wise course for weathering the menopausal years with a minimum of discomfort.

Some women sail through menopause with no noticeable trouble, and there are those who claim that Chinese acupuncture treatments have made the difference. All women can take comfort in the fact that most of the unpleasant symptoms of menopause accompany the transition period and last no more than about two years, even in the most difficult cases.

During this transition, the following teas can be useful.

They're not hot flashes, they're power surges.
—Anonymous

Vitex Infusion

Vitex agnus-castus—also known as chasteberry—is a highly touted herbal therapy for many menstruation-related conditions, especially menopause. Its effect on the body is gradual and cumulative, so the therapy is most useful when used over a period of months.

$1/2$ ounce dried vitex berries, crushed
1 cup water, barely boiled

Place the berries in a teapot, pour the boiling water over them, cover, and steep 15 minutes. Strain and drink 1 cup three times daily, sweetened with honey, if desired. (Tinctures and capsules are also available. Consult a reputable herbalist for more information.)

Sweet Relief

This licorice and sage blend is often recommended by herbalists for women experiencing hot flashes and night sweats. It makes a good nightcap for menopausal women. Licorice tea is not recommended, however, for women with high blood pressure, pregnant women, or women with fibroids.

$1/2$ teaspoon dried licorice root
1 teaspoon dried sage leaves
1 cup water, barely boiled

Place the herbs in a teapot and pour the boiling water over them. Steep for 15 minutes, strain, and sip slowly while warm.

MENSTRUAL PAIN

For some women, "cramps" rate at the top of their list of all-time biggest pains—not counting childbirth, of course. Cramps are caused by the uterine contractions that initiate and maintain the monthly flow. For reasons that are not well understood, some women find these contractions extremely painful, while others barely notice them. If you are among the sufferers, your pain-relieving options are not confined to dependence on muscle-relaxing drugs that may impair mental alertness or sap your physical energy.

For starters, take a look at your diet. Some doctors believe that constipation can severely aggravate menstrual pain, so be sure to eat plenty of fiber-rich foods, particularly in the days leading up to your period. Whole grains and fresh fruits and vegetables are terrific sources of fiber. On another dietary note, consuming lots of sweets or salty foods before and during menstruation may contribute to especially bad cramps in some women.

Getting enough calcium in the diet—along with magnesium, which aids calcium absorbtion—can have the long-term effect of reducing menstrual discomfort. Consider taking a cal-mag supplement—to minimize menstrual pain and lessen your risk of osteoporosis.

Many women apply warmth to relieve severe cramps. A heating pad on the abdomen or a hot bath may work for you, as well. Try putting a handful or two of soothing herbs like lavender or chamomile in the bath water. I find the aroma alone quite relaxing. Simple rest is also good therapy, particularly on the first day of your period. Declare it your monthly personal holiday, and stay off your feet as much as possible.

It is important during menstruation to replenish lost fluids. Water, fresh fruit and vegetable juices, and warm herbal teas are excellent beverages for this purpose. Stay away from iced drinks and cold foods like ice cream, which slow the circulation and may increase cramping.

Rest and Relax Blend

This tea can help with minor menstrual cramps. It has a pleasant taste and a nice fragrance that I find soothing.

1 teaspoon dried chamomile flowers
1 teaspoon dried raspberry leaf
1/2 teaspoon dried yarrow
1 cup water, barely boiled

Place the herbs in a teapot. Pour the boiling water over them, cover, and steep 15 minutes. Strain and sweeten with honey, if desired. Sip slowly while warm.

Cramps Defense

Valerian is an age-old tranquilizer. Some herbalists associate excessive use with depression, nervous exhaustion, and mental instability, so it is considered wise to drink no more than 1 cup a day for no more than a few days in a row. Peppermint is added for its antispasmodic properties, and for a pleasant taste.

1/4 teaspoon dried valerian root, crushed
2 teaspoons dried peppermint leaves
1 cup water, barely boiled

Place the herbs in a teapot. Pour the boiling water over them, cover, and steep 15 minutes. Strain and sweeten with honey, if desired. Sip slowly while warm, in 1/2-cup doses.

NAUSEA

Certain people seem equipped with "iron stomachs" that blithely withstand all kinds of mistreatment, from deep-sea fishing trips to triple pepperoni pizzas—even both at the same time!

Most of us, however, feel a little queasy now and then. Nausea might be caused by motion sickness when traveling by car or boat, undigested food that stays too long in the stomach, or a flu bug that brings us a host of miserable symptoms. Women in their first trimester of pregnancy are prime candidates for "morning sickness"—regular bouts of mild to severe nausea.

Whatever its cause, nausea is telling us our stomachs are distressed. One of the things distressed stomachs do is empty themselves. If the urge to vomit strikes, don't fight it. This is often your quickest route to feeling better.

Ginger is a tried-and-true nausea reliever and is one herbal remedy frequently recommended by mainstream doctors. Travelers can carry crystallized ginger in a handbag or pocket to suck when nausea strikes. The ginger tea discussed below is a good remedy if you are at home with the tea kettle handy.

If you feel nauseated for more than a couple of days, get yourself to the doctor. Meanwhile, take care of yourself by sipping clear liquids like broths and water (sips are easier on the stomach than long draughts of liquid). Avoid carbonated beverages—the bubbles can be unsettling to touchy tummies. If you feel like eating at all, make it small portions of bland carbohydrates such as plain crackers or dry toast. Chew very well before swallowing and wait a minute or so between bites to see how your stomach is handling the recently introduced food.

The following teas can also be part of your self-care routine while you ride out the queasiness.

Ginger and Clove

Ginger and cloves both go back a long way in herbal medicine and continue to be frequently prescribed for stomach complaints. Strong ginger beverages such as this one are not suitable for women in the early months of pregnancy.

1 inch of fresh ginger root
4 whole cloves, crushed
1 cup water, barely boiled

Coarsely chop the unpeeled ginger and place it in a teapot. Crush the cloves with a mortar and pestle or the broad side of a knife and add to the pot. Pour the boiling water over the herbs, cover, and steep 10 minutes. Strain and sweeten with honey, if desired. Sip slowly while warm.

Peppermint Anise Tonic

Peppermint and anise are other long-time stomach remedies. Drink this tea to alleviate nausea, or after vomiting to soothe and strengthen the stomach.

2 teaspoons dried peppermint leaves
1/2 teaspoon dried aniseed
1 cup water, barely boiled

Place the herbs in a teapot and pour the boiling water over them. Cover and steep 10 minutes. Strain and sweeten with honey, if desired. Sip slowly while warm.

SORE THROAT/HOARSENESS

For most of us, a sore throat results from a bacterial or viral infection that may herald an impending cold or flu. There are other causes, however. A sore throat and/or hoarseness can result from exuberant cheering, loud singing, or other types of vocal strain. People with severe hay fever or pollen allergies sometimes experience a sore throat among their symptoms.

Occasionally, a sore or irritated throat may be the result of sleeping in an overheated or very dry room. A night-time humidifier may help. Dry throats can also benefit from steam inhalation. Boil a quart or two of water and pour it into a large bowl. Add a handful of eucalyptus leaves (any species) or lavender flowers and allow the water to cool off for a few minutes. Drape a towel over your head and bend over the bowl, allowing the towel to drape loosely around the bowl, to create an enclosed tent. Breathe the steam in gently through your mouth. Adjust your distance from the bowl to regulate the heat of the steam.

A simple salt water gargle is soothing. Dissolve some salt in a small amount of warm water and gargle gently, but do not swallow. Just enough to make the water taste salty is sufficient—$1/2$ teaspoon to 1 cup of water is about right. The salt water gargle may be used as often as once an hour.

Of course, resting the throat is part of sore throat therapy. Use your voice as infrequently as possible, and when you do speak, speak softly. If a sore throat persists for more than a few days, or if it is accompanied by a fever, it is wise to consult a doctor.

Whatever the cause of your sore throat, any of the following home remedies may be useful.

Singer's Friend

Singers, actors, and others who use their voices professionally have been known to relieve hoarseness by using this remedy.

2 tablespoons fresh lemon juice
2 teaspoons honey
1 teaspoon minced garlic
1 cup water, barely boiled

Place the lemon juice, honey, and garlic in a cup. Add the boiling water and stir until the honey dissolves. Do not strain. Sip slowly while warm.

Raspberry, Elder, and Thyme

This tea has a wonderful, soothing fragrance. For optimum enjoyment, inhale deeply while sipping it.

1 teaspoon dried raspberry leaves
1 teaspoon dried elder flowers
1/2 teaspoon dried thyme
1 cup water, barely boiled

Place the herbs in a teapot. Add the water, cover, and steep 10 minutes. Strain and sweeten with honey, if desired. Sip slowly while warm.

Herbal Gargle

Soothing herbal gargles will stay fresh at room temperature for a few days. Strain out the herbs after a few hours and store away from direct heat or sunlight, preferably in a dark glass bottle.

1 teaspoon apple cider vinegar
1 tablespoon of any of the following dried herbs:
    crushed fenugreek seeds, lavender flowers, sage leaves,
    or peppermint leaves
1 cup water, barely boiled

Boil the water and combine it in a teapot with the vinegar and herbs. Cover and steep 5–10 minutes, then strain and cool. Gargle the brew 1 tablespoon at a time, every few hours, as needed.

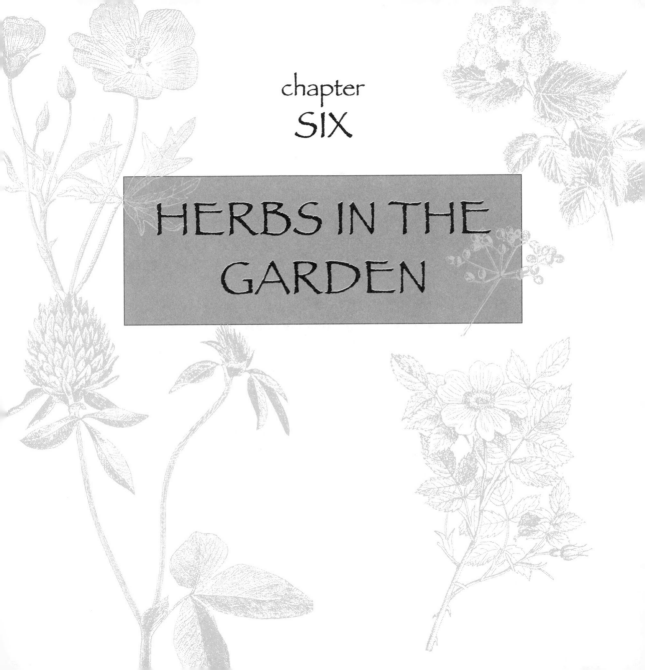

chapter
SIX

HERBS IN THE GARDEN

In a very real sense, all of nature is a garden—a beautiful ecosystem in which plants, minerals, insects, and animals interact in the dance of life. For discussion purposes, however, we generally define a garden as a human-cultivated grouping of plants, with clear borders separating it from the wilds. Growing a garden allows us to emphasize in the landscape our favorite plants. It is a way to customize Eden.

If you feel convinced you've no talent for gardening, take heart. Because herbs are essentially wild plants, many can establish themselves and flourish for years with absolutely no assistance from us. Some, in fact, are classified by cranky gardeners as "#%^*@ weeds!" because they cling so tenaciously to life, even when they are not wanted.

So, if you have only a very small spot of dirt with adequate sun exposure—even if you are limited to pots on a patio or cramped windowsill—you can have a very satisfying herb gardening experience. It takes some level of interest, of course, and a few seeds or seedlings. If you possess these, in a single morning you can plant a small herb garden that will lavish its gifts upon you for years to come.

Herb Gardens of Old

There is a long and colorful history preceding our own gardening endeavors. As we learn about the plants and how to grow them, we become the recipients of an ancient body of knowledge. We may choose to disregard some of the traditional wisdom—about soil preparation or companion planting, for instance—but we are nevertheless beholden to the gardeners of the past.

For many centuries, the garden was an essential part of every household. Plants provided food, of course, but were also sources of fibers, dyes, cosmetics, seasonings, and medicines. These latter categories of plants—jointly referred to as the herbs—were often gathered in the wild, but were also cultivated in home gardens.

In addition to their utilitarian value, gardens have always been places of refreshment and reflection, entertainment and enjoyment. The lady's pleasure garden, sometimes called a "paradise garden," was much the rage during the Middle Ages. It typically included fountains and ponds, grasses cultivated as lawns, trees to provide fruit and shade, and the lavish use of aromatic flowering herbs.

These days, not every home has a garden. But a few things never change. We humans continue to rely on the plants for our very lives. And gardens are still places that can rejuvenate our senses, fill us with wonder, and open our hearts to the beauty of the world.

Herb Garden Design

Tea herbs can be planted throughout the garden—as borders, hedges, and ground covers as well as dominant flowering shrubs. They offer a vast diversity of colors, fragrances, and foliage and flower forms that provide inspiration for the creative garden designer.

Some gardeners group plants according to the color of their foliage or flowers. Others choose to group plants by category—culinary, medicinal, flowering, fruiting. My preference is to spread plants around and mix them up, rather than growing them in controlled rows and beds. The result is exuberantly beautiful to me and seems closest to nature's design. Different considerations concern different gardeners. Design possibilities for your herb garden are practically unlimited.

Some famous gardens, dedicated largely or exclusively to herbs, were documented for posterity and can be studied, even recreated, by today's home gardeners. A trip to any well-stocked library can put these time-tested planting guides at your disposal.

Garden Companions

Many gardening reference books discuss "companion planting," the grouping of particular plants near one another for their mutual benefit. Some classic garden companions are:

Balm with all vegetables

Basil with tomatoes

Borage with strawberries

Chamomile with onions

Dill with corn, cabbage, or lettuce

Garlic with roses

Sage with cabbage or carrots

Thyme with eggplants, tomatoes, or potatoes

A Note About Medicinal Plants

Ideally, we could all harvest medicinal herbs in the wild, where nature has planted them. Wild plants compete for sunlight, water, and nutrients in the soil, so only the strongest survive. Home garden conditions tend to make life easier for these plants, and they become mellower as a result.

It is wise to provide the most ideal conditions possible for our food crops to create the sweetest and most tender produce, but we want our medicines potent. This is why plants harvested in the wild—termed *wildcrafted*—are considered by herbalists to make the best medicinals. Their beneficial properties are thought to be strongest and most concentrated.

Many of the important medicinal herbs, however, occur naturally in limited geographical areas. What's more, most of us don't possess the expertise required to accurately identify wild plants, and mistakes can be dangerous, even deadly. Gathering herbs from our gardens is quick, safe, and easy. So, though wildcrafted medicinal herbs may be the best, home cultivated ones are very good, too.

Of course, you will not have success with tropical plants if you live in a predominantly cool climate, and vice versa. But every home gardener can grow a wide selection of beneficial plants. (And what we can't grow, we can purchase in dried form. See page 116 for names and addresses of mail-order herb suppliers.)

Your First Herb Garden

Below are my recommendations for easy-to-grow herbs for the absolute beginner. They are not particular about soil, but they do prefer decent sun exposure. I recommend planting them in pots and placing the pots in an exposed spot on the south side of your house for best results. If you live in a hot summer area, water your potted plants regularly when temperatures soar.

I prefer wooden or terra cotta planters to the plastic kind. Plastic pots are fine if that's all you've got, but my plants seem to "breathe" better in wood or clay. I think they look better, too, in weathered barrels or earthy terra cotta than they do in slick black or green plastic.

To create a little flower is the labour of ages.
—William Blake

108

Regular potting soil, available at every nursery, is fine for herbs. They like good drainage, so a little extra sand or vermiculite in the mix wouldn't hurt. Most herbs won't ever *require* fertilizing, though they respond well to a little compost gently worked into the soil now and then.

Please refrain from the use of chemical fertilizers, pesticides, and weedkillers. Most herbs are not prone to insect infestation, so why run the risk of poisoning the air, soil, and water around your home with harsh chemicals? I am a firm believer in organic gardening methods for herbs and every plant in my garden. Every gardener ought to consider herself the latest in a long line of earth stewards, nurturers of life. Chemical fertilizers, pesticides, and herbicides are not consistent with this role.

The ABCs of Planting

To plant your first herb garden, acquire some containers and good, healthy soil, and buy seeds or vigorous-looking seedlings from a reputable nursery with knowledgeable staff. You don't want to plant oregano and find out later you've got marjoram.

Prepare each pot by filling its bottom with rocks or chunks of broken terra cotta pottery. This will create an airy space for drainage at the bottom of the pot. Add enough soil to fill the pot up to an inch from the rim. Saturate the soil with a gentle stream of water from the hose and set the pot aside for a few minutes to drain thoroughly. Pick up the pot and gently tap its bottom on a sturdy surface to settle the soil, then add more soil to bring the level back up to an inch or two from the rim.

At this point, if you are sowing seeds, follow the instructions on the back of the packet. If you are planting nursery seedlings, dig a hole in the soil with your hands about the same size as the container the plant came in. Hold the container at an upside down 45-degree angle and gently tap it against a hard surface to release the plant from the pot. Hold your hand around the base of the plant as you do this so you will be sure to catch it as it is dislodged.

If the plant's roots are twisted together in the shape of the pot, the plant is root-bound and needs a little extra help before planting. Gently spread and separate some of the roots, which will give them a head start in their search for new soil. If the plant's roots are loose and well covered with soil, try to disturb them as little as possible.

Place the plant in the hole you have dug and gently press dirt in around its roots. You should cover the plant's main stem with soil to the same level it was covered in its previous pot. Press gently but solidly all around the base of the plant to firmly imbed it in the soil. Water the pot again, using a very thin stream to avoid disturbing the soil, and leave to drain.

Seeds will probably need to be watered daily with a fine spray if the weather is warm. Check the surface of the soil and water whenever it feels dry. With young plants, as well, check their progress daily. Water when the soil is dry to the touch one inch below the surface, or when the plant seems to look wilted.

If the container is large enough, you can combine a few different herbs in it. Most herbs coexist happily and may even benefit each other.

Here is a list of herbs that are easy on the beginning gardener. They will add visual beauty and wonderful fragrances to your life, along with inspiration for the teapot and the skillet.

Borage	Oregano
Calendula	Parsley
Catnip	Peppermint
Chamomile	Rosemary
Lavender	Sage
Lemon balm	Thyme

What is a weed?
A plant whose
virtues have not
been discovered.
—Ralph Waldo
Emerson

Harvest and Storage

Leaves and Flowers

Before a plant flowers, its volatile oils are concentrated in the leaves. Therefore—since an herb's aroma, flavor, and medicinal value are contained in these oils—it is preferable to harvest leaves and stems before plants bloom. Of course, blossoms,

seeds, and roots are harvested later in the season when the desired plant parts have fully developed. For best flavor, pick flowers when they are at their loveliest and most aromatic.

Herbs should be harvested when plants are dry but not wilted. Early morning after the dew has evaporated is an excellent time for gathering flowers, leaves, and stems. Use sharp snips or scissors for harvesting leafy herbs, and cut through the stem at a point just above a set of leaves. This type of pruning ensures vigorous new growth on the plant.

After harvest, remove any damaged or discolored parts. Gently rinse the herb with water, shake off the excess, and dry with clean cotton towels. If you will be using the herb in its fresh form, remove the leaves from the stems and place the measured amount in your tea pot. Fresh herbs not used immediately may be wrapped in a damp paper towel and placed in a plastic bag in the refrigerator for up to a few days. Some large-leafed herbs—such as basil or mint—may be left on the stem and placed in a jar of water. Place this small green bouquet on a countertop out of direct sunlight. The leaves will stay fresh for 2–3 days and will perfume the kitchen nicely.

If the herb is not to be used fresh, it should be prepared for drying immediately. Remove any damaged or discolored leaves. Tie the branches of small-leafed herbs together in small bunches. The leaves of larger-leafed herbs are usually removed from the stems and spread out to dry in a shallow layer on a fine-mesh wire rack. You may wish to cover the rack with a light towel or cheesecloth to keep flying insects and dust off the herbs.

Herb bundles or racks should be placed in a warm area out of direct light for drying. A basement, shed, or garage is ideal as long as conditions are dry and not too cool. In wet or cold weather, it is better to dry herbs in the house, where air temperature and humidity are controlled.

Hang bunches of herbs from the rafters or from wall hooks. Drying racks should be positioned on a table or other surface well off the floor to avoid the possibility of insect infestation.

Most herbs will air dry in this manner in 1–3 days, depending on weather conditions. Some coarser-leafed varieties—such as comfrey—can take a week or longer. Check the drying process daily by crushing a leaf or two of the herb between your fingers. Herbs should crumble easily and feel bone-dry. When leaves or flowers are completely dried, transfer them to glass or ceramic containers labeled with name and date. Store the jars in the pantry or a kitchen cupboard away from direct light, heat, and moisture.

Life must blossom
like a flower,
offering itself to
the Divine.
      —The Mother

Seeds

If you wait too long in the season to harvest seeds, they will dry on the plant and begin to drop. At this stage, the seed heads are very delicate and tend to explode in every direction when handled. So select a day for harvest when the seeds are no longer green but are just barely beginning to dry.

Harvest seeds after the morning's dew has evaporated but before it is too hot. Use sharp snips or scissors to cut off the entire seed head, gently transferring it to a paper bag. Snip a few holes in the sides of the bag and hang the bag in a dry, warm place out of direct sunlight. (Alternately, you may use a muslin bag, which will not need air vents cut into it.)

Seeds will drop from the seed heads when they are thoroughly dried. No more than a week is usually required, depending on temperature and humidity level. Transfer dried seeds to labeled jars, mark with the date, and place in the pantry or a cool, dry cupboard.

By the way, any dried herb seeds that are not used for teas or cooking during the fall and winter can be planted in the spring to begin the new year's crop.

Roots

Roots are best harvested in mid-season, when they are well-developed but not overly large and tough. Gently dig or pull up the plant, remove the green parts, rinse with water, and towel dry. Trim off and discard any tributary roots growing from the main tap root and chop the root finely. Spread the root pieces out on a fine-mesh wire rack, cover with a light towel or cheesecloth, and store as for leaves and flowers.

Depending on the size of the pieces, roots will take from 7–10 days to dry thoroughly. Roots are properly dried when they become hard and crush to a dry powder. Store the dried roots in labeled and dated jars in the cool pantry, and use as is or ground to a powder just before using.

Mail-Order Resources for Herbs and Herbal Supplies

There are a great many herb farms and other herbal businessesin the United States. You may find out about those in your area by asking around at farmer's markets or your local nursery.

If you are unable to find a local source for herbs, mail-order is a good alternative. The farms and firms listed below offer a wide variety of supplies for the budding herbalist, such as plants, dried herbs, teas, and other essentials. They all offer catalogs of their mail-order products, free or for a nominal cost.

Brown's Edgewood Gardens
2611 Corrine Drive
Orlando, FL 32803

Dry Creek Herb Farm
and Learning Center
13935 Dry Creek Road
Auburn, CA 95603

East-West Herb Products
65 Mechanic Street, Suite 103
Red Bank, NJ 07701

Forever Meadows Herb Farm
Box 646
Cornish, ME 04020

Goodwin Creek Gardens
P.O. Box 83
Williams, OR 97544

Lily of the Valley Herb Farm
3969 Fox Avenue
Minerva, OH 44657

Logee's Greenhouses
141 North Street
Danielson, CT 06239

Mountain Rose Herbs
Box 2000
Redway, CA 95560

Nichols Garden Nursery
1190 South Pacific
Albany, OR 97321

Rasland Farms
Route 1, Box 65
Godwin, NC 28344

Shady Acres Herb Farm
7815 Highway 212
Chaska, MN 55318

Shepherd's Garden Seeds
6116 Highway 9
Felton, CA 95018

Story House Herb Farm
Route 7 Box 246
Murray, KY 42071

Renaissance Acres
4450 Valentine
Whitmore Lake, MI 48189

Suggestions for Further Study

I found the following books and periodicals useful in my research for this work. Many other informative and inspiring herbals are also available, as a visit to any bookstore or library will reveal. Enjoy your studies!

Books

Griggs, Barbara. *Green Pharmacy: A History of Herbal Medicine*. New York: Viking Press, 1981. A fascinating look at the evolution of medicine and pharmacology.

Kowalchik, Claire and Hylton, William H., Eds. *Rodale's Illustrated Encyclopedia of Herbs*. Emmaus, PA: Rodale Press,   1987

Lust, John. *The Herb Book*. New York: Bantam Books, 1974. A comprehensive herbal text, with detailed information about the plants.

Marcin, Marietta Marshall. *The Herbal Tea Garden*. Pownal, VT: Storey Communications, 1993.

Ody, Penelope. *The Complete Medicinal Herbal*. London: Dorling Kindersley Limited, 1993. A practical guide with beautiful color photographs of many plants and the medicinal preparations made from them.

Tierra, Michael. *The Way of Herbs*. New York: Pocket Books, 1990. An overview of the herbal approach to health and healing, with information about Chinese and Western herbs.

Periodicals

Two quarterly herb journals:

Sage Advice
3741 Old Charlotte Pike
Franklin, TN 37064

HerbalGram
American Botanical Council
P.O. Box 201660
Austin, TX 78720

A bi-monthly glossy magazine:

The Herb Companion
Interweave Press
201 E. 4th Street
Loveland, CO 80537

INDEX

These are not exact equivalents: they have been slightly rounded to make measuring easier.

LIQUID MEASUREMENTS

American	Imperial	Metric	Australian
2 tablespoons (1 oz.)	1 fl. oz.	30 ml	1 tablespoon
1/4 cup (2 oz.)	2 fl. oz.	60 ml	2 tablespoons
1/3 cup (3 oz.)	3 fl. oz.	80 ml	1/4 cup
1/2 cup (4 oz.)	4 fl. oz.	125 ml	1/3 cup
2/3 cup (5 oz.)	5 fl. oz.	165 ml	1/2 cup
3/4 cup (6 oz.)	6 fl. oz.	185 ml	2/3 cup
1 cup (8 oz.)	8 fl. oz.	250 ml	3/4 cup

SPOON MEASUREMENTS

American	Metric
1/4 teaspoon	1 ml
1/2 teaspoon	2 ml
1 teaspoon	5 ml
1 tablespoon	15 ml

WEIGHTS

US/UK	Metric
1 oz.	30 grams (g)
2 oz.	60 g
4 oz. (1/4 lb)	125 g
5 oz. (1/3 lb)	155 g
6 oz.	185 g
7 oz.	220 g
8 oz. (1/2 lb)	250 g
10 oz.	315 g
12 oz. (3/4 lb)	375 g
14 oz.	440 g
16 oz. (1 lb)	500 g
2 lbs	1 kg

OVEN TEMPERATURES

Farenheit	Centigrade	Gas
250	120	1/2
300	150	2
325	160	3
350	180	4
375	190	5
400	200	6
450	230	8